# TOGETHER LOCALLY

A handbook for local churches
seeking to work together

with a foreword by
the Revd Dr Kathleen Richardson

Jenny Carpenter

CTE (Publications)
Inter-Church House
35-41 Lower Marsh
London SE1 7RL

ISBN 1 874295 13 1


© Jenny Carpenter 1998
Cover design by Ray Liberty
Printed by Tyndale Press (Lowestoft) Ltd
Published by CTE (Publications)
Inter-Church House
35-41 Lower Marsh
London SE1 7RL

# TOGETHER LOCALLY

# CONTENTS

# FOREWORD

To be local is to be real. We are becoming increasingly aware that ecumenical work is about relationship - fellowship (*koinonia*) in the Gospel which issues in the full range of mission. It is in the local setting that relationships and deeper friendships are most likely to grow. It is also in the local setting that difficulties and frustrations are most likely to be felt. The local situation is the testing ground for ecumenism, and it can also be the power house for change. We are well aware that any national/denominational plans and ideas have to justify themselves at the 'grassroots' or the 'coalface'.

I have known Jenny Carpenter personally for many years in both her ecumenical work and her involvement in the Methodist Connexion. I know her commitment to the ecumenical movement and I value her knowledge of the local scene - councils of churches, and nowadays Churches Together groupings. There can be no-one more qualified to produce a handbook for *local churches working together*.

I am therefore delighted to welcome the appearance of this book which must be essential reading for everyone who cares about ecumenical and collaborative working in local areas.


The Revd Dr Kathleen Richardson

President of Churches Together in England

For contact names of those involved in specific initiatives referred to in this book, write to Churches Together in England (North & Midlands) Office, Crookes Valley Methodist Church, Crookesmoor Road, Sheffield S6 3FQ.

# INTRODUCTION

Where we are matters to us. Our locality is unique and it is here that we are called to live out our Christian discipleship, even though some of us live on a larger map.

I am a 'places' person. It is one of the greatest joys of serving as a Field Officer of Churches Together in England that I have a licence to travel and meet Christian groupings of all kinds **on their home ground.** Unless I have some knowledge of a place, I feel inhibited about offering guidance. In my years working as a town planner I spent more time out of the office than in it, making 'site visits' or absorbing and mapping what constituted the genius of the place.

There is a wonderful passage in which the prophet Ezekiel is taken *"by the strong hand of God but in bitterness of spirit"* to proclaim the word of the Lord to the exiles in Babylon. But first he has to share their experience. *"And there, where they were living, I sat among them for seven days overwhelmed."* [1] It is only when he has identified with them and caught their mood of desolation that the Word of the Lord comes to him and he speaks out.

This identification with the local and particular is evident, too, in the life of Jesus. God chose to reveal himself in human form – he became incarnate, bone of our bone and flesh of our flesh. Jesus ate and drank, laughed and cried and above all **took notice**. His awareness of the local environment and *mores* is one of the most remarkable features of the gospel record. In some ways his experience was limited, but it was always intense. His earthly life was lived **locally** but his life, death, resurrection and ascension were of **cosmic** significance.

What is local can be seen to be 'real'. This is true of the experience of churches working together:

"...... ecumenism has been experienced by ordinary people in local churches. They have learned about other traditions, worshipped together, grown in understanding, learned how to live with differences, learned that they do not possess the whole truth, built new friendships and partnerships, engaged in service of their neighbourhood together, raised money for peoples far distant and generally found new perspective on life. This is not theory. This has happened and involved innumerable ordinary people in a new communion. It has been part of a vast learning experience." [2]

Some feel challenged to find a way of relating and working that expresses the Churches Together concept but are still struggling to do so. Local initiatives have been published and shared through county ecumenical newsletters and through *Pilgrim Post,* produced six times a year by Churches Together in England, to inform and encourage others. [3]

From 15-17 April 1996 the Group for Local Unity of Churches Together in England held a consultation entitled 'Together Locally', whose two-fold aims were:

i) to promote quality relationships between churches in localities;

ii) to produce a handbook for local Churches Together groupings.

Thanks are expressed to those who formed the Planning Group for the Consultation: Colin Brady, Shirley Coombes, Christine Craven, David Newman, Bill Snelson and Cecil White. Thanks also to the writers of preparatory papers for the working groups on the themes of Chapters 7 to 15, those who acted as group facilitators and scribes and especially to Flora Winfield who gave the keynote address which set all our sharing in a challenging and wide ecumenical context. Many stories representing disappointment and failure as well as success were shared. A selection of these and other more recent ones with an eye to geographical balance are included here.

I am especially indebted to the Writing Group who met residentially: Shirley Coombes, Anne Doyle, Roger Nunn, Martin Reardon and Mary Wetherall to advise on structure and style whose detailed comments have helped to improve the book – as has Bill Snelson whose pruning-hook was well employed in the later stages. Thanks to Judith Lampard who provided the content of Chapter 6 and has overseen publication, Gill Stedman who produced publication-ready copy, and Colin Davey for his proof-reading skills. The biggest thank-you must go to Gill Wells who chivvied and encouraged me to keep working on the book, providing many cups of fairly-traded coffee, produced the various drafts in legible form and prepared the index.

This handbook is offered as guidance and resource to all those who are seeking to live as Churches Together in their neighbourhood or town. Recognise the particularities of your place as well as the peculiarities of its people, but don't let that inhibit initiatives. *"Can anything good come out of Nazareth?"* was a popular saying in New Testament times. Just look what did! Not everywhere can be an Abingdon, a Dronfield or a Horsham. As we listen together to what the Spirit is saying to the churches in **our** place, we shall hear both rebuke and encouragement.

If this handbook helps you to move from co-operation to commitment in your own situation, prompts you to strengthen your links with your county body or encourages you to share the story of your experiments, frustrations and joys more widely, it will be serving its purpose.

Jenny Carpenter

-------------------------------------------------------------------------------------------

## FOOTNOTES:

1. Ezekiel 3.15b (New International Version).

2. Quoted with permission from John Sutcliffe's Sabbatical Study, Part 4 *Ecumenical Theological Education,* shared by the Moderator of Churches Together in England's Group for Local Unity, the Revd Sheila Maxey, at the Consultation described in the next paragraphs of the Introduction.

3. *Pilgrim Post* – for a free sample copy and subscription details, contact the CTE South Office, Baptist House, 129 Broadway, Didcot, Oxon, OX11 8XD.

# 1. THE CALL TO LOCAL UNITY

## 1.0  Deeper Faith and Wider Love

1.1 The inspiration of all inter-church sharing is found in the *koinonia* fellowship that binds the persons of the Trinity and the *kenosis*, self-emptying of Jesus in his incarnation, ministry and passion.[1] The gospel is not our private property. We serve a crucified and risen Lord who is a universal Saviour. Our concern must be to develop a deeper faith that fuels a wider love – expressed in the everyday life of individual believers, local churches and the world for which Christ died.

## 2.0 Principles for working together

2.1 As early as 1952 the World Faith & Order Conference at Lund posed the question to the Churches whether they "should not act together in all matters except those in which deep differences of conviction compel them to act separately" (Lund Principle).

2.2 In 1964 the British Faith & Order Conference at Nottingham reaffirmed that Lund challenge while adding the rider "there is no virtue in doing things together which we ought not to be doing anyway". This means that local churches are required to establish **priorities** in what they are seeking to do together. No-one can do this for them. It must be a local decision. It will need to be an informed decision – based on the strengths and possibilities and needs of the churches and of the area they serve. The priorities must be agreed by the normal decision-making body in each local church and then decisions taken about which to tackle together. It is important neither to be so overwhelmed by what true commitment might entail that we are paralysed into doing very little together, nor to insist on integrating everything all at once!

2.3 In 1967 in a report *Planning the Ecumenical Parish* a specially commissioned group exploring new church patterns in Northamptonshire, formulated what came to be known as the Corby Principle – "The Church should not do on its own that which it can do with the community." Ecumenism is concerned with the whole of life – not just an evidently 'churchy' agenda.

2.4 These three principles, then, need to be referred to constantly as churches work together in their locality.

> ✶ **Churches should act together in all matters except those in which deep differences of conviction compel them to act separately – Lund Principle.**
>
> ✶ **There is no virtue in churches doing things together which they ought not to be doing anyway – Nottingham Principle.**
>
> ✶ **Churches should not do on their own what they can do with the community – Corby Principle.**

## 3.0 Gift and Calling

3.1 The search for Christian unity was one of the main concerns of the Second Vatican Council. The Encyclical *Unitatis Redintegratio* stated "The desire to recover the unity of all Christians is a gift of Christ and a call of the Holy Spirit".[2]

9

Catholics were asked to reach out in love to all other Christians, working actively to overcome in truth whatever divides them from one another. This same Encyclical called for spiritual ecumenism – a "change of heart and holiness of life, along with public and private prayer for the unity of Christians" which it regarded as "the soul of the ecumenical movement".

## 4.0 **Churches Together**

4.1 Then at Swanwick in 1987 at the climax of the Interchurch Process, the four-nation 'Not Strangers but Pilgrims' conference declared "It is our conviction that, as a matter of policy, **at all levels and in all places,** our churches must now move from co-operation to clear commitment to each other, in search of the unity for which Christ prayed and in common evangelism and service of the world".[3]

4.2 "At all levels and in all places" means that we, as local congregations, are challenged to allow the Christian imperative of reconciliation and unity to inspire our life alongside fellow Christians in our own town, our own village.

4.3 We can no longer be content to live in separation. We need each other's gifts and insights. We need to use resources wisely. We need to find ways of working with men and women of vision and goodwill in our communities, whether avowedly Christian or not. We need to discover together how, in our particular place, something of the sacrificial love at the heart of the gospel can be expressed and shared. We need together so to live and act that Christ can be perceived more readily in our community. "See how these Christians love one another!" is often exclaimed in tones of sarcasm. Can it, in our place, begin to be said with appreciation and warmth?

4.4 "If we can demonstrate that diversity need not mean division, and that we can be self-affirming without being other-denying, defining ourselves in inclusive, not exclusive, terms then we shall be a sign of the Kingdom for whose coming we all pray."[4]

4.5 We need in our local church or congregation to discover ecumenism "as a dimension of everything that we do".[5] The call to unity comes as a continuing spur to conversion to what may seem new ways of thinking, new ways of being, new ways of acting. We may slip back into denominational or parochial or narrowly congregational attitudes. But, unless we work at discovering the reality of the unity that already binds us as Christian churches and seek to make that unity more visible and tangible, we will be failing to live out the fullness of our Gospel calling. If **we** don't attempt it in our locality, who else will express it and put it into effect?

------------------------------------------------------------------------------------------

**FOOTNOTES:**

1. Keynote Address by the Revd Flora Winfield, given at the Group for Local Unity's Consultation "Together Locally", 15/17 April 1996.

2. *Unitatis Redintegratio,* 1964.

3. The Swanwick Declaration can be found in *The Next Steps for Churches Together in Pilgrimage*, otherwise known as the Marigold Book, published in 1989 by British Council of Churches and the Catholic Truth Society. Copies available from Churches Together in England offices. It can also be found in *Called To Be One*, CTE (Publications) 1996.

4. Churches Together in Cornwall response to *Called To Be One*.

5. Marigold Book p3.

COMING TOGETHER

## 2. GETTING STARTED

### 1.0 Starting from where we are

1.1 Happily, some ecumenical relationships and desire for Christian unity exist everywhere in England. We are all at different places along the 'C' scale.[1] The aim is to move along that 'C' scale from Conflict > Competition > Co-existence > Co-operation > Commitment > Communion.

1.2 Although the 1987 Swanwick Declaration spoke of the Churches moving from co-operation to commitment, in many places we have hardly moved from co-existence to co-operation. So – we mustn't try and run before we can walk. It is safer to take only one step at a time.

1.3 It doesn't matter whether the desire for Christians to work together more closely is expressed by clergy or by lay people, so long as opportunities are provided for the vision to be caught and shared.

### 2.0 Where does the initiative and energy come from?

2.1 Different kinds of people may spark the vision:

* The **pray-ers**. Those who live close to Christ are likely to be inspired by his prayer in John 17. In any locality there are likely to be some people who pray with regularity and passion for Christian unity.

* Those with practical experience of two or more denominations – especially **Interchurch families** (defined as those where husband and wife belong to different denominations.)[2]

* Those who have **good experience** of ecumenical life in another part of the country.

* Those who have lived abroad and developed some sense of the **World Church** (e.g those who have first-hand knowledge of United/Uniting Churches in the Indian sub-continent).

* Those who have first-hand experience of gross injustice and poverty and have a **passion to right wrongs** in the name of Christ.

* Those who **work with young people** – in church or school and are aware how difficult it is to instil Christian values and to make the gospel appear relevant to the younger generation.

### 3.0 Those who must also be involved

3.1 Whoever has the vision first, it is important that certain key people catch it.

* Those who deeply **love their locality**. "Oldest inhabitants" can often turn out to be powerful allies for an inclusive approach which will address the real needs of the neighbourhood or town.

★ Unless those having responsibility for the **material aspects of church life** are prepared to ask the ecumenical question, you are not likely to get very far.

★ Leaders will inevitably include the **clergy,** who are in the strongest position to inspire, encourage and lead others.

## 4.0 The Ministers' Meeting

4.1 Many clergy value opportunities for getting to know opposite numbers in neighbouring churches. Often they can be a source of personal support and friendship.

4.2 Where clergy are themselves members of a denominational team who meet on a regular weekly or even daily basis (as in many Anglican Teams) for worship and planning, it may be helpful to offer informal membership to other local clergy so including the ordained and authorised leaders of all the Christian churches in that locality.

4.3 A regular meeting of clergy/pastors who are learning to pray, do theology and share their understandings of the community/ies that they are seeking to serve is likely to enable progress along the 'C' scale. Without meeting, mutual understanding and trust cannot grow.

4.4 This presupposes operating at a local level. A regular clergy meeting that is too large will not allow all to make input. Individuals then tend to absent themselves. 'I won't be missed!'

4.5 It is always difficult to match diaries. Some of the clergy/pastors may be part-time. This is likely to be true of the pastors of most black majority churches, who are often in full-time secular employment, as well as non-stipendary ministers in other churches. In some places clergy meet for prayer and breakfast so that those with other 'day jobs' are not excluded.

4.6 So – getting a clergy group meeting regularly is a good way to maintain contact and develop some sense of common Christian service and purpose for the locality.

## 5.0 Local Initiative

5.1 Another way of getting started may be for one church to invite other churches to a **social** occasion. This can then be followed up by a jointly organised event. The occasion could be a patronal festival, the centenary of a building or the opening of a new church hall.

5.2 A flower festival that is held simultaneously in each church on a common theme can develop a sense of unity and also be a way of encouraging non-churchgoers to cross the threshold of the church.

## 6.0 National or Regional Initiative

6.1 The initiative may come from beyond the locality. Many ecumenical groupings have been fostered by a desire to join in a national or regional initiative. It was the *People Next Door* programme for ecumenical groups in 1967 which was the impetus for forming or enlivening many local councils of churches. *What on earth is the Church for?* in Lent 1986 involved a resurgence of local ecumenism. Every other year there is a nationally produced Lent Course published under the auspices of the Council of Churches for Britain & Ireland, which is a golden opportunity for small groups of Christians to meet, study, pray and act together.[3] Such groups can engender deep friendship and a desire to learn more about other churches. They can also be a spur to effective gospel-sharing and service to the locality. Christian Aid initiatives and One World Week provide a similar framework for joint learning, working and witness.

## 7.0 Exploring the nature and needs of the locality

7.1 The unity of the Church is not just an end in itself. Unity and mission belong together. The Forum of Churches Together in England (July 1997) said that "This communion is a relationship of love and trust between the followers of Christ ........ This love binds all the followers of Christ together in the Holy Spirit, moves us to worship and leads us to action in obedience to the call to share in the mission of God." But how is that mission to be described? The word is used in so many ways in different traditions.

The Forum went on to suggest that the following formulation is helpful in describing the characteristics of that mission :

   ✶ *proclaiming the good news of the kingdom*

   ✶ *teaching, baptising and nurturing new believers*

   ✶ *responding to human need by loving service*

   ✶ *seeking to transform unjust structures of society*

   ✶ *striving to safeguard the integrity of creation and sustain and renew the life of the earth.*[4]

These characteristics of mission have been used as a focus for parish renewal in dioceses in the Church of England such as Oxford and Chelmsford. Ecumenical bodies at different levels are now discussing whether they could be a useful guideline and challenge for their work. Many things that we need to be doing ecumenically could be summed up in that one word 'mission', understood in the holistic way set out above. One advantage of this mission approach is that it can bring together Christians and churches who would have said that they were not interested in 'ecumenism'.

7.2 The churches need to focus on **priorities.** In small communities Christians are used to working together on the parish council or the village hall committee. In urban situations it can be very heartening to discover who are the other Christians in the street or the block of flats. Mapping the churches and their regular congregations can be an encouragement and also an alarm bell – if it becomes apparent that there are significant areas from which **none** of the churches is drawing in any numbers. This discovery could be the beginning of an exploration **together** of the make-up of the area, a visiting programme, talking to the local council about incidence of social deprivation.[5]

This could enable the churches to identify and give priority to some initiative in which they might share so as to develop a sense of community there.

## 8.0 Unity and Diversity

8.1 Some people are motivated strongly by the love of Christ experienced in their own lives. Others are galvanised into action by perceived need or opportunity. Local churches are likely to include those who exercise authority and those who resist or challenge it. There will be extroverts and introverts, activists and those who want a quiet life; there will almost certainly be more women than men. There will be people who are pushing for change and experiment and others concerned to stay within known limits of the tried and tested.

8.2 What has become apparent over recent years is that **within** any one denomination there will be as many tensions and differences in emphasis as there are **between** denominations. We **all** have to struggle to hold together in unity while rejoicing in a great breadth of diversity. It is often perceived that to enter into formal inter-church relationships is in some way going to compromise strongly cherished beliefs and threaten the unity of the local congregation.

8.3 These formal inter-church relationships may take a variety of forms. In many places this will be a local Churches Together grouping. In some villages where there is only one church building there may be a Declaration of Ecumenical Welcome and Commitment.[6]

Where there are only a couple of churches, there may be some reciprocal representation on decision-making bodies. Where relationships are close a Local Ecumenical Partnership may be justified. Local churches may covenant to work closely together while retaining distinct worshipping congregations or a single congregation partnership may be formed where appropriate.[7]

------------------------------------------------------------------------------------------------

### FOOTNOTES:

1. The original 'C' Scale was propounded by John Nicholson when working as ecumenical officer for the British Council of Churches in the late 1970s. It has since had 'conflict' added to it. (See 'From Conflict to Communion' by Colin Davey, *One in Christ*, Vol 29, 1993 - 1, p81.)

2. See also Chapter 9, 6.0.

3. Details of Lent Courses available from CCBI Publications, Council of Churches for Britain & Ireland, Inter-Church House, 35-41 Lower Marsh, London SE1 7RL.

4. This is based on the Five Marks (or Strands) of Mission, which have come to us from the world-wide Anglican Communion and were a particular emphasis of the Lambeth Conference, 1988.

5. Churches Information for Mission, an agency set up in 1997, is aiming to provide detailed computerised mapping for any geographical area in England based on published census information and statistical material provided by the major Churches.

Churches Information for Mission, c/o The Revd Roger Whitehead, The Churches Co-ordinating Group for Evangelisation, The Manse, 116 High Street, Harrold, Bedford, MK43 7BJ.

6. *Guidelines for A Declaration of Ecumenical Welcome and Commitment* authorised by and available from the Church of England's Local Unity Committee, Council for Christian Unity, Church House, Westminster, SW1P 3NZ.

7. See *Travelling Together*, Welch & Winfield, CTE (Publications) 1995.

## 3. BUILDING A FRAMEWORK

### 1.0 **Formal or informal?**

1.1 Relationships are more basic than structures; but structures can be a safeguard. Of course we can work informally – but such arrangements have a habit of falling apart when a key person moves away or when someone new comes in and doesn't know the formalities of the informality! This handbook is about securing a framework for working together.

### 2.0 **Drawing up a Constitution : See Appendices II(a)(b) and III(a)(b)**

2.1 Each church should be asked to appoint a representative who knows what is likely to be feasible and acceptable. These representatives will form a steering group. There must be frequent checking back with the decision-making structure of each church. It will take **longer** than if one church is working on its own but one church taking the initiative and later inviting others to join is not acting truly ecumenically. Clergy changes during the planning period must not be allowed to halt the momentum or be an excuse for a church to withdraw support.

2.2 In most parts of England there is an intermediate/county body which can offer advice through its Ecumenical Officer. The name of your County Ecumenical Officer can be obtained from Churches Together in England offices.[1] Be realistic about the timetable, and note the dates of meetings of decision-making bodies and then work through the questions in Appendix I(a) or II(a).

2.3 If possible, adopt the BASIS of Churches Together in England.

*Churches Together in England unites in pilgrimage those Churches in England which, acknowledging God's revelation in Christ, confess the Lord Jesus Christ as God and Saviour according to the Scriptures, and, in obedience to God's will and in the power of the Holy Spirit commit themselves:*

> *– to seek a deepening of their communion with Christ and*
>
> *with one another in the Church, which is his body; and*
>
> *– to fulfil their mission to proclaim the Gospel by common*
>
> *witness and service in the world*
>
> *to the glory of the one God, Father, Son and Holy Spirit.*

It is of the essence of the Churches Together concept that churches **recognise the common core of their faith and their call to a common task** which is expressed in this Basis.

The integrity of bodies which are non-credal must be respected. Provision has therefore been made at national level for the Religious Society of Friends to become a member of Council of Churches for Britain & Ireland and of Churches Together in England without being required to subscribe to the Basis.[2]

In the Constitution the churches' mutual commitment will be expressed as AIMS AND OBJECTS which must secure the following practice :–

to pray for each other and for unity locally and worldwide;

to be honest with each other and face disagreements openly;

to share how as churches we see ourselves and our task;

to see how much of our ordinary church agenda can be worked on with partner churches;

to trust one church to act in the name of all where appropriate;

to live out our common calling to share in God's mission.

It is necessary to talk through what the aims and objects should be. Appendix II sets out Constitutional Guidelines for a Neighbourhood Churches Together grouping with Questions to ask when drafting the constitution. Appendix III sets out further suggestions for an 'umbrella' Churches Together grouping which has the same boundary as a local authority area and which principally will have a co-ordinating role. (See also Chapter 12).

2.4 Careful thought must be given to what **area** can meaningfully be covered. Any existing or potential adjacent church groupings should be consulted about where they feel they belong.

2.5 The smaller the number of churches involved, the simpler the structure can be.

2.6 Churches and Christian fellowships which are not members of Churches Together in England may well be prepared to join a local Churches Together grouping and should be involved from the start. (See Questions in Appendix II(a) and III(a)). If there is doubt or unease about the appropriateness of including a particular church or fellowship, the County Ecumenical Officer should be consulted.

2.7 **Membership** should refer to participating churches or interest groups. Individuals appointed to serve are **representatives** of participating members. Confusion will be avoided if this distinction is clearly drawn.

2.8 A list of Churches Together in England member churches is given in Appendix II. This does not **limit** the churches that can belong to a local Churches Together grouping, not least because many congregations are constitutionally independent without being part of a national association or church. Other churches need to agree/affirm the Basis.

### 3.0 Commitment of each local church

3.1 It is **very important** that a decision in principle to form a Churches Together grouping is agreed by the normal decision-making body for each local church (PCC, Church Meeting etc). Where an 'umbrella' Churches Together grouping is being formed, such decisions should be taken by the deanery(ies), circuit(s), United Reformed District, Baptist Association, etc.

3.2 It is **equally important** that the same decision-making body agrees the wording of the Constitution. It is not enough for the appointed representatives to agree it.

3.3 Inform the wider church that you are doing this (County Ecumenical Officer, Denominational Ecumenical Officers, Rural Dean ..... ).[3]

3.4 The main difference between many of the local councils of churches which have been in existence for a long time and a carefully thought-through Churches Together in X is that the latter is fully rooted in the whole life of each member church. It is of crucial importance that the leadership and the decision-making body of each local church are committed to the enterprise and continue to take responsibility for it.

## 4.0 Launching Churches Together in Xtown: Where, When, Who and What

4.1 The following are important:

* It will help if something significant has already been achieved together
* Make an occasion out of the launch of the local Churches Together grouping
* Think carefully about the precise date and time of the launch
* Pentecost is a good season for such a celebration
* Involve as many people as possible and make sure that all the local clergy can attend
* Invite representatives of the local Council
* Invite denominational church leaders (bishops, chairmen and moderators etc.)
* Read out greetings from absent leaders
* Ensure County Ecumenical Officer and denominational ecumenical officers can come
* Invite a speaker with experience of wider ecumenism
* Write your own liturgy – but draw on available resources.[4] You might even commission a new hymn!
* Invite and advertise widely in the local press and on local radio

--------------------------------------------------------------------------------------------

**FOOTNOTES:**

1. Churches Together in England: Inter-Church House, 35/41 Lower Marsh, London SE1 7RL. Telephone: 0171 523 2009/2010.

2. See Appendix II(b), 5. MEMBERSHIP & Footnote 3.

3. See 4.1 below and Chapter 4.

4. Examples of orders of service for the launch of a local Churches Together are available from the CTE Field Officers:

Field Officer (South), Baptist House, 129 Broadway, Didcot, Oxon, OX11 8RT. Telephone: 01235 511622.

Field Officer (North & Midlands), Crookes Valley Methodist Church, Crookesmoor Road, Sheffield S6 3FQ. Telephone: 0114 268 5171.

## 4. LINKING UP

### 1.0 Local Unity is not enough

1.1 Ecumenism, by its very nature, can never be content to be only local. In Greek *oikoumene* means the whole inhabited earth. The Third Assembly of the World Council of Churches meeting in New Delhi in 1961 produced the following statement about the nature of unity:–

"We believe that the unity which is both God's will and his gift to his church is made visible as all in each place who are baptised into Jesus Christ and confess him as Lord and Saviour are brought by the Holy Spirit into one fully committed fellowship, holding the one apostolic faith, preaching the one Gospel, breaking the one bread, joining in common prayer, and having a corporate life reaching out in witness and service to all and who at the same time are united with the whole Christian fellowship in all places and all ages in such ways that ministry and members are accepted by all, and that all can act and speak together as occasion requires for the tasks to which God calls his people."[1]

Every local grouping which has some minimal constitution is urged to tie in to something wider. Most of the local church congregations will themselves be part of a deanery, a circuit, a district or regional grouping within their own denomination. For some of them this belonging is profoundly important: for others much less so. All recognise their place in the Universal Church – the fellowship of believers on earth and in heaven. The fact that the urge toward unity is known as the ecumenical movement, which has its own dynamic, indicates a refusal to be confined.

1.2 It may be useful to picture ecumenism like concentric circles. So if the local ecumenical relationships and activity are in the centre, the next ring out may correspond to an 'umbrella' grouping for the town or city, the one beyond it to the Intermediate Body and so on. (See diagram below). It will be important to ensure that there are inbuilt links between adjacent rings and in some cases to the next two rings so that information and help can readily flow in both directions.

## 2.0 'Umbrella' Groupings of Churches Together in a large town or city

2.1 In major towns and cities it will usually be helpful for groupings of Churches Together in a neighbourhood or small town to affiliate to a Churches Together group embracing a geography equivalent to a unitary or district local authority area.[2]

2.2 Many so-called 'umbrella' Churches Together bodies are formed with representation both from wider denominational units (e.g. deanery and circuit) and from neighbourhood ecumenical units (e.g. neighbourhood Churches Together groups and Local Ecumenical Partnerships). Where appropriate they will be able to co-ordinate neighbourhood activities and have a major role in communicating information. Issues of wider than neighbourhood concern – such as matters to do with local authority services, health care, major new population growth etc. – can be tackled at the appropriate level.

## 3.0 The Intermediate Body

3.1 Whereas before 1990 local councils of churches were encouraged to affiliate to the British Council of Churches, now they or their equivalent are urged to affiliate to the appropriate Intermediate Body (usually at the level of the county), such as Churches Together in Shropshire or Sussex Churches Together. The name and address of the Secretary/Ecumenical Officer of that body can be obtained from Churches Together in England offices.[3]

3.2 All local Churches Together groups and 'umbrella' ones (see below) should be in regular touch with their Intermediate Body. The Intermediate Bodies seek to resource and encourage all appropriate ecumenical activity at local level and give guidance in good practice.[4] Many of them arrange evening or day conferences when officers and representatives of local Churches Together groupings can meet and exchange ideas.

3.3 Some of the Intermediate Bodies have representation from local Churches Together groups on their Council, Executive or Enabling Group. Nearly all of them have a regular newsletter (monthly, quarterly or twice-yearly) in which articles about the development of ecumenical working at local, county and wider levels is shared.

*Pilgrim Post* [5] is another publication which keeps readers informed of ecumenical news and can be a source of inspiration for local unity.

3.4 The Secretary should inform the County Ecumenical Officer of changes in names and addresses of officers and send minutes and (if possible) agendas. Most County Ecumenical Officers will be glad to attend meetings occasionally and to help with suggestions for speakers, preachers or people with training skills.

Most Intermediate Bodies set a modest affiliation fee for local Churches Together groups. This fee will help to pay for a newsletter (normally at least one copy for each member church), regular mailing to the Secretary and the expenses of sending someone 'representative of local unity in the county' to the Forum of Churches Together in England, which is held in July every other year.

## 4.0 Taking ecumenical thinking and experience into denominational life

4.1 It is important that each denomination knows about the links being forged with other local churches. Ecumenical plans and experiences should be shared in denominational meetings. This is a valuable way of encouraging others to be more open to fellow Christians. All of us experience pressure to embrace denominational initiatives. If we are taking local ecumenism seriously we may find that we have to challenge demands to follow a narrowly denominational agenda, where this would prejudice commitments already made. On the other hand denominational life and patterns cannot be ignored as they necessarily run deep. They need to be shared with others if we are to increase understanding and share one another's riches.

## 5.0 Wider ecumenism

5.1 Individuals within a local Churches Together group may belong to or have links with specific ecumenical groupings – e.g. Iona Community, Association of Interchurch Families, Fellowship of Prayer for Unity, Bible Society, YMCA, Focolare, National Retreat Association etc.[6] Each of these is a source of prayer and worship material which will widen and unify church life in the locality. Young adults (and others) who are hanging on to worship in a local church by the skin of their teeth may be given new energy and vision through Iona or Taizé worship.

---

## FOOTNOTES:

1. WCC New Delhi Report, p116.

2. See Chapter 12.

3. See Footnotes 1 and 4 to Chapter 3.

4. *This Growing Unity: A Handbook on ecumenical development in the counties, large cities and new towns of England* Roger Nunn, CTE 1995.

5. *Pilgrim Post* – for information about subscriptions or for a free sample copy, write to Churches Together in England's Didcot office: Baptist House, 129 Broadway, Didcot, Oxon, OX11 8RT. Tel. 01235 511622.

6. See list of Bodies in Assocation of Churches Together in England on p99, and other useful addresses on p104.

## 5. DECIDING TOGETHER

### 1.0 Decision-making in Local Churches Together

1.1 The 'Churches Together' way is to entrust major decision-making on ecumenical activity to the normal decision-making bodies of each participating church. Representatives at local Churches Together meetings will share the concerns and activities of each member church, and consider which of them might properly be engaged in by all the churches. Any proposals coming from the local Churches Together meeting will then be taken back to each of the decision-making bodies of the member churches (Parochial Church Council, Church Meeting, the Catholic Priest with his Pastoral Council, etc.) and only when they all (or at least the vast majority) agree will the local Churches Together grouping put their proposals into effect. In this way the decisions are properly the decisions of the local Churches Together, and not simply of their representatives at a meeting. They are therefore much more likely to obtain widespread support from all the participating churches, and a proper ownership by the members of their congregations.

1.2 This should be reassuring to any who fear that being part of a local Churches Together grouping is going to compromise cherished beliefs and threaten the unity of the local congregation. Where one member church does not approve an action, it has the opportunity, indeed the responsibility, to insist on its right to dissociate itself from any specific action taken by Churches Together in X. When the dissenting church explains why it is not able to support some particular action or event, it is probable that partner churches will be encouraged to modify their own approach or at least to argue more clearly why it is justified.

1.3 However, this way of working could become clumsy and slow. To overcome this danger, Churches Together meetings have to be very carefully planned to fit in with the calendar of the meetings of the decision-making bodies of all the participating churches. Member churches' decision-making meetings should be encouraged, so far as possible, to take place at roughly similar times in the year; and local Churches Together meetings should be spaced out to occur at different times. This would enable local Churches Together meetings to receive from member churches their suggestions, requests and matters for ecumenical consideration. These could be considered at the local Churches Together meeting which could then send its recommendation to the next decision-making meetings of all the member churches. The decisions of the churches could then be registered and acted upon at the following meeting of the local Churches Together.

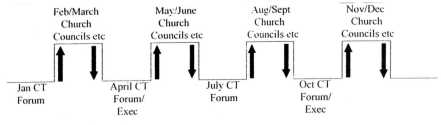

1.4 Such a programme requires considerable discipline both on the part of the church meetings and of the local Churches Together meetings. Church meetings need to consider the ecumenical implications of all the items on their agenda.

Local Churches Together meetings need careful preparation and a clear agenda (which indicates items for decision and items for information only), disciplined chairing and speedy preparation and circulation of minutes to make clear who has the responsibility for carrying out each decision registered at the meeting.

If all this is to work, the dates of meeting need to be planned a year ahead.

1.5 One of the most important differences between how most local councils of churches used to work and how local Churches Together are intended to work today concerns how they reach decisions.

1.6 Local churches used to send their representatives to meetings of the local councils of churches, which then often took decisions on ecumenical activities by means of a majority vote. This enabled decisions to be taken quickly, and where the representatives were well-briefed about their respective churches' attitudes and policies, ecumenical activity could often be well supported and effective. In too many places however the representatives were unable to obtain the full support of their churches for what had been decided, and ecumenical activities tended to become an optional extra, additional to the normal life of the denominations, and supported only by enthusiasts.

**2.0 Importance of Priority Setting**

2.1 Two of the major enemies of a successful Churches Together grouping are rush and the failure to set priorities. It is often not easy for local churches to agree priorities. Failure to do so can result in the local Churches Together trying to do too many things and doing none well. Time spent sorting out and agreeing priorities will bring dividends. It is a good exercise for churches to discuss both individually and together what their priorities are for the next few years; and it is far more important to engage in a few priorities together than in a multitude of peripheral activities.

2.2 Another major issue is what **sort** of things churches do together. It is easier to do new things together – things that none of the churches has done before. It is important, though, that churches are also challenged to do together the things that they have previously been doing separately.

3.0 **Joint Meetings**

3.1 In a local Churches Together which does not have too many participating churches it may be possible occasionally to have a joint meeting of either the whole or part of each church's decision-making body to consider priorities and long-term strategy.

4.0 **Relationship with Ministers' Meeting**

4.1 The relationship of a meeting of clergy and ministers (often called a ministers' fraternal), and the local Churches Together grouping needs to be thought out and clarified. Clergy and ministers are influential in the decision-making of all our churches, but they are much more influential in some than in others. It is vital therefore that clergy and ministers play a full part in the local Churches Together grouping. The ministers' meeting can be very useful in helping to prepare for a local Churches Together meeting and for helping to follow up and implement the decisions it has reached. The fraternal should not normally attempt to reach those decisions itself, let alone to change them. If it does it may well alienate large groups of lay people who will then not feel committed to the life and activity decided upon.

## 5.0 Representatives of Other Churches on decision-making Bodies

5.1 Ideally, decision-making bodies should have representatives of other churches present when they meet. Some Synods, whether of the CofE Diocese, URC Province or Methodist District invite official observers from other denominations to attend – with the right to speak, though not usually to vote. It is less common to replicate this at the level of the Deanery, URC District and Methodist Circuit and even more unusual at Parochial Church Council, Church Meeting or Church Council, but this is where the local church agenda is thrashed out!

## 6.0 Decision-making in the denominational setting

6.1 It is only when ecumenical awareness permeates denominational life that churches really work together. It is worth setting out the ecumenical questions which are now basic to church agendas on **Merseyside** and are being taken up more widely. They underline the ecumenical dimension to all church work by applying certain questions to each item of the agenda. They were first adopted by the **Liverpool Methodist District** Synod in May 1992 and circulated to each circuit and local church.

* *What information or request relating to this business has been received from any of our ecumenical partners?*
* *What information or request relating to this business do we refer to any of our ecumenical partners?*

*At the end of each agenda the following questions should be asked :–*

* *What work do we offer to any of our ecumenical partners on their behalf?*
* *What work do we ask any of our ecumenical partners to consider undertaking on our behalf?*
* *What matters for general discussion do we refer to the Local Advisory Group, Local Covenant and/or Local Council of Churches or to the Merseyside and Region Churches Ecumenical Assembly, the Regional Sponsoring Body or any other regional ecumenical body?*

6.2 The Liverpool District was well aware what it was doing. It was recognised that the application of these questions to any agenda would significantly weight that agenda with an ecumenical bias. This was quite deliberate because, to quote from the original Guidelines "we are becoming increasingly aware, particularly in the Merseyside region which includes the whole of the Liverpool District, that partnership with other traditions not only makes sense, but is an integral part of our total response to the Decade of Evangelism."

6.3 Chairs and Secretaries were asked to reproduce the questions on the head of every printed agenda, and also to flag those agenda items which clearly had ecumenical implications. It would be in order for any member of the meeting to raise the first two questions in relation to other items on the agenda.

6.4 The Liverpool Diocesan Synod adopted the same ecumenical questions for use by its Bishop's Council and Diocesan Committees and the URC Mersey Province warmly embraced the principles.

6.5 The Methodist District Ecumenical Committee monitored the use and effect of the questions, and an abbreviated form was subsequently approved by the Synod. It reads as follows:–

*During the course of our business we need to consider the ecumenical aspects of everything we do. Specifically, is there anything we can offer our ecumenical partners? and is there anything we can learn from them? We recommend that circuits and local churches appoint an ecumenical watchdog to ensure that these considerations are borne in mind.*

6.6 This concept has proved very challenging not only to local Methodist churches and circuits but to their ecumenical partners – especially where relationships were not very strongly developed. There have been at least three effects. One is to highlight the ecumenical implications inherent in many 'routine' local church decisions. The second is to create a sense of frustration and impatience with the time taken by ecumenical consultation, and the role of the local Churches Together grouping can be critical here (see 1.1, 1.2 and 1.3 above). The third is that when there is serious ecumenical consultation, better decisions are taken and acted on in a more effective way.

COMING TOGETHER

## 6. TECHNICALITIES NOT TO BE OVERLOOKED

### 1.0 Charity Registration

1.1 Churches Together in England (nationally) is a registered charity, but its charity registration number may **not** be used by local groups as these are independent of it. It may be that your local Churches Together does not need to be registered as a charity if you do not employ staff or own property. It is important to look carefully at the pros and cons if you consider registering. The Charity Commission issue a number of useful leaflets available from **The Charity Commissioners, St. Albans House, 57-60 Haymarket, London SW1Y 4QZ.**

### 2.0 Data Protection

2.1 The Data Protection Act of 1986 is restricted to computer files, and intended to safeguard people's interests. It may not be necessary to register if you only keep people's names and addresses on the computer for the purpose of sending information to them. In this situation, the people concerned must be informed that their names are held for this purpose and asked if they object. Details are available from **The Office of the Data Protection Registrar, Wycliffe House, Water Lane, Wilmslow, Cheshire SK9 5AF.**

### 3.0 Copyright

3.1 Local Churches Together groupings should make sure that they meet all the requirements of Copyright Law, if they wish to reproduce hymns or prayers, etc.

### 4.0 Accounts Audit or Inspection

4.1 Local Churches Together groupings should have their accounts inspected each year. In large organisations (with annual income of over £100,000) the audits **must** be done by a qualified auditor, who is a member of a professional association. For small organisations, those which are unincorporated and do not receive a substantial grant, it is usually sufficient that the amounts are inspected by someone who is competent and not directly involved with the organisation.

### 5.0 Insurance

5.1 Under the Employer's Liability (Compulsory Insurance) Act 1969, all employers have a duty to insure against any claims by workers for injury or disease. The insurance certificate must be displayed in the work place. However their insurance does not cover management committee members, volunteers or service uses, and sometimes groups need to consider whether public liability insurance may be needed. This covers injury, loss or damage caused to any person as a result of an organiser's negligence. Where Churches Together groupings are organising particular events in a church, other building or grounds, it may be that they are covered by the owner's insurance. This should never be taken for granted, and the situation should always be clarified before the event.

Professional advice should be sought – sometimes this is available through the member churches. Sometimes it is appropriate for one church to act on behalf of the **whole group.**

## 6.0 **Meetings in a public place, marches and processions**

6.1 It is necessary to inform the local police in good time when such events are being planned. The local authority should be consulted about processions to see if any local by-laws apply. Special insurance cover may be advisable. The Council of Churches for Britain and Ireland publishes advice before General Elections on the legal requirements surrounding meetings of parliamentary candidates.

## 7.0 **Child Protection**

It is important to bear in mind the implications of the Children Act, when working with children and young people. *Safe from Harm* (HMSO) is the Home Office code of practice for safe-guarding the welfare of children in voluntary organisations in England and Wales. A number of churches have produced their own helpful guidelines.


**The best advice: always take proper legal and financial advice from those qualified to give it. Never assume that the situation is the same as it was many years ago – the law constantly changes!**

# *LIVING AND WORKING TOGETHER*

## 7. CHURCHES UNDERSTANDING EACH OTHER

### 1.0 Differing Understandings

1.1 Understanding one another is basic, though difficult. It doesn't happen overnight. Sometimes there is a rapport between individuals from different Christian traditions that enables them to speak of the things which really matter to them. It is only when dialogue of this kind is possible that there will be a break-through in inter-church relations.

1.2 It is a valid criticism of some inter-church groupings that although embracing several denominations they share a particular theological stance or understanding, e.g. liberal or evangelical/charismatic. It is important to recognise that there is particular value in working alongside people whose spirituality and tradition is very different from one's own.

### 2.0 Important Factors

Some of the factors to be aware of are:

* Definition by difference
* The way we understand/use the Scriptures
* Clergy/lay roles, especially in decision-making
* Sociology, age structure and ethnic mix of each local congregation
* Whether a church is rooted in the locality or more widely 'gathered'
* Religious history of the area
* Understandings of baptism and membership
* Teaching and practice with regard to the eucharist
* Church structures – independency

    – hierarchy

    – interdependence

    – connexionalism
* Ethical stances – e.g. pro-life, genetic engineering, pacifism.
* Use of language – do we use the same words to mean different things?

### 2.1 Definition by difference

Because of the particular religious history of England, churches are defined by their differences, e.g. 'non-conformist', 'non-Catholic'. 'They' are different from 'us'. It is important to recognise that 95% of Christian belief and practice is held in common. Some local churches have produced a 'mission statement' to encapsulate how they see themselves and their role. A comparison of these could be very enlightening in the process of developing greater understanding.

## 2.2 The way the Scriptures are understood and used

There may be churches who would style themselves 'evangelical' who find it difficult to work with those whom they perceive as 'catholic'. How literally should the Scriptures be taken? It is possible to take the Scriptures seriously without being fundamentalist. What is properly contained in the Bible? What weight is accorded to Scriptural principles? The modern Roman Catholic practice of encouraging personal bible reading and of giving greater weight to the reading of Scripture and the homily should encourage evangelicals to associate with Roman Catholics. Most Christians acquire 'antennae' for discerning where others stand on this clearly important issue. They wait for the green or red light – can I work with them or not? It can be disconcerting talking to Christians who intersperse their conversation with Biblical quotations if one is not used to it! Other Christians will not necessarily be persuaded to change their stance on the understanding and use of Scripture. It is healthy to share some conversation on this topic. Respect must be accorded to each other's firmly-held convictions, while daring to suggest that it is possible for people of widely differing views to work together.

## 2.3 Clergy/lay roles, especially in decision-making

Beware of caricaturing other churches. The respective roles of clergy and laity vary with denomination and the idiosyncrasies of the local church. In some Protestant churches the minister/pastor is far more of an autocrat than is the priest in most Roman Catholic or Anglican parishes. All denominations are thinking through how everyone can play an appropriate part and discover his or her own gifts and exercise a distinctive ministry within and beyond the church. The priorities of ordained ministers will vary. Attendance at meetings comes higher up the list for some than for others. Free Church people who pride themselves on their lay involvement are often amazed to discover the widespread use of lay people as eucharistic ministers and catechists in Catholic parishes.

It is important to explore how decisions are taken and where authority lies in each church. In none of our churches can we force people to support events or throw themselves vigorously into some new initiative. In the last resort lay involvement in the life of the local church is **voluntary**, whatever the official teaching may say. People can vote with their feet.

If the clergy are luke-warm about ecumenism, it is bound to affect the development of a local Churches Together group.

## 2.4 Sociology, age-structure and ethnic mix of each local congregation

These factors will affect the confidence of the congregation and its ability to take the pulse of the community in which it is set. Some churches attract a significant number of teenagers and young adults – and it is well known that like attracts like. Others may cater particularly well for elderly people.

There is a tendency to feel happier with people perceived as sharing one's own kind of social/geographic background. How varied is each local church? Is there a tendency for ecumenism to appeal only to people of a certain level of education?

In many places friendship between individual Christians from the various churches is more evident than a growing sense of fellowship between churches. There is a danger of cultivating an ecumenical elite who delight in working together but cease to be representative of or influential within their own congregation.

## 2.5 Whether a church is rooted in the locality or more widely 'gathered'

Church of England parishes are usually reasonably compact, except in thinly-populated rural areas, while Roman Catholic parishes tend to be much larger, and worshippers will travel considerable distances to attend Mass, though they may be reluctant to do so for other forms of worship or for meetings. Because of the Circuit system, Methodism is able to maintain a large number of small congregations, most of whom live locally and identify with the neighbourhood, but may not have as much resource or energy as some other churches. Baptist and United Reformed Churches are based on the concept of the gathered congregation – those who, committed followers of Christ, covenant together to worship and help each other to live in obedience to Christ. There is much emphasis on individual responsibility for sharing the Gospel. The Church of England emphasises its role to care for everyone in the parish, Christian or not. There may be a strong identification of the parish church with any church schools, official bodies and with the whole community.

## 2.6 Religious history of the area

All Church of England churches that pre-date the Reformation were once Roman Catholic worship centres. This needs to be taken to heart! Is there a history of ongoing Catholic resistance after the Reformation? If so, this will be celebrated with pride by local Catholic parishes, who will treasure their martyrs and value the continental links which kept Roman Catholicism alive during the centuries of persecution. Can denominational pilgrimages or celebrations of saints and martyrs be transformed into ecumenical celebrations?

Quakers have stories to tell of individuals of tremendously strong personal convictions who refused to compromise their beliefs.

Many Free Churches were built in an attitude of defiance of the Established Church. Particularly in country areas, the church/chapel divide can still run deep. The Free Churches in the nineteenth century saw themselves in direct competition with the Church of England and with each other. Attitudes of competition do not readily change to co-operation, let alone commitment.

Churches need to take on board each other's history but also to allow ecumenical memories to be healed. There is a need to express pride in our past, without carrying bitterness. Most people have had some encounter with another Christian tradition which has reinforced their prejudices or scarred them in other ways. The need for reconciliation between the Churches was a major theme during 1997, explored at the European Conference at Graz in June and featuring at the Churches Together in England Forum in July. It applies at all levels.

## 2.7 Understandings of baptism and membership

Some churches practise only believer's baptism and not infant baptism. Beware of seeing this as a 'problem' if this is not your tradition. Believer's baptism has positive value. It underlines how vital is the insistence that each individual must come to a personal faith in and public commitment to Christ. Some churches which practise infant baptism have a policy of baptising children of parents who are not regular churchgoers. This 'open baptism policy' expresses the belief that the grace of God is offered to all, irrespective of response. Both these understandings need somehow to be honoured. It will be helpful in the context of the local Churches Together group to explore the understandings and practices of individual churches.[1]

## 2.8 The Eucharist: teaching and practice

There is much evidence of convergence in understandings of the eucharist.[2] Many of our authorised liturgies are remarkably similar. However it is at the eucharist where Christians should be fully at one with Christ and with each other that our denominational divisions are at their most evident and most painful. Because the eucharist is so central to the life of the Church, there is an obligation on a local Churches Together group to provide opportunities for understandings to be shared. Chapter 8 deals with joint eucharistic worship.

## 2.9 Church structures

It is important to understand something of the basis on which each of the churches is structured. Though most have elements of several, **one** of these principles is likely to predominate: independency, hierarchy, interdependence and connexionalism. For example, the connexional principle has been fundamental to Methodism, and the circuit structure makes demands on each local congregation, which in turn can benefit from mutual care. A tension is sometimes evident between local ecumenical involvement and full commitment to other churches in the circuit.

Churches with episcopal structures will find themselves expected to play their part in diocesan training or study programmes and may be torn between diocesan loyalty and a desire to share in an ecumenical initiative.

Those churches which have an understanding of the local congregation as guided and empowered by the Spirit to take its own decisions can commit themselves strongly to working ecumenically locally, but a bad experience can also lead to an equally firm decision to withdraw. "What do you understand by church?" has rightly been seen as a key question in *Called To Be One*.[2]

## 2.10 Ethical stances

In many places, local churches have found themselves able to make common cause over issues such as homelessness and poverty. It has to be recognised, however, that Christians hold divergent views on issues such as birth control, abortion, genetic engineering, pacifism and gambling.

It seems reasonable to suggest that a local Churches Together group may:

* campaign together on some issues
* provide practical care and assistance in response to others and
* create opportunities to thrash out the ethical principles underlying the differing views which exist.

## 2.11 Use of language

Many churchy words have different denominational connotations, e.g. Deacon, Presbytery, Bidding Prayer, District, Offertory, Evangelism, Evangelisation. To a remarkable extent, each denomination has evolved its own language. It is not easy to communicate with each other (in either sense). Even the religious jargon which is shared is largely impenetrable to those outside the Church. Fear of giving offence can be a reason for reluctance to get involved with other churches. Common courtesies should be observed, e.g. modes of address, both spoken and written.

2.12 All the foregoing factors will influence how ready and able local churches are to work together in different aspects of their corporate life. They could also be the basis for an afternoon or evening 'workshop'.

## 3.0 Difference can be valuable

3.1 One of the great joys of *What On Earth is the Church For?*, the Lent Course in 1986, was that ecumenical house groups discovered not only how much the churches had in common, but also that the differences were both important and **valuable.** To be different was not necessarily to be wrong! This massive step forward in recognising the value of diversity has been an increasingly important factor in ecumenical relations.

## 4.0 Others help us to understand ourselves

4.1 When others question us about our faith and practice these often become clearer to us too.

> In a local council of churches, a series of meetings on the Roman Catholic sacraments was in progress. The URC minister was explaining how he understood 'Penance'. At the end a Roman Catholic couple said – "That makes sense, to see it as a response to God's forgiving grace. We have never really understood it before!"

4.2 The recent upsurge in house groups – denominational and ecumenical – has challenged Methodists in many places to rediscover the significance of the Class Meeting in their own tradition.

## FOOTNOTES:

1.  *Baptism, Eucharist & Ministry, World Council of Churches, 1982.*

    *Called To Be One*, CTE (Publications) 1996, note particularly Appendix B.

    *Believing and Being Baptised*, Baptist Union of Great Britain, 1996.

    *Baptism & Church Membership*, CTE (Publications) 1997.

2.  *Baptism, Eucharist & Ministry*, see Note 1. above.

    *Called To Be One*, see Note 1. above. Note particularly Appendix C.

**Other books to enable better understanding of certain traditions –**

*Black Christians: Black Church Traditions in Britain*, A Resource Pack produced jointly by the Centre for Black & White Christian Partnership & Westhill RE Centre, Selly Oak Colleges, Birmingham, 1995.

*Dying to Be ONE: English Ecumenism: History, Theology and the Future*, David Butler, SCM 1996.

*The Handbook of The International Ministerial Council of Great Britain.* A Uniting Body for the Black Pentecostal Churches, IMCGB, 1990.

*The Liturgy after the Liturgy: Mission and Witness from an Orthodox Perspective* Ion Bria, WCC Publications, 1996.

## 8. CHURCHES WORSHIPPING AND PRAYING TOGETHER

### 1.0 Centrality of Worship

1.1 Worship is clearly central in the life of every Christian and of every local church. Because of that it must have a key part to play in the pilgrimage to church unity. Corporate prayer has been an important part of the ecumenical movement over the past one hundred years.

### 2.0 Worship – unity or division?

2.1 Worship reveals the disunity of the Church. Roman Catholic teaching on eucharistic sharing is often mentioned as an example of the divisions that remain between the churches. It is, however, worth reflecting on some of the other examples of times when people find it difficult to worship together. 'Charismatic', 'new age', 'evangelical', 'Toronto blessing', 'bells and smells': these are some of the names and labels given to forms of worship that are important expressions of faith for some Christians and yet disliked (and often feared) by others. It is easy to be dismissive of styles that are unfamiliar, too structured, too 'free', too noisy or difficult to follow. We may not like such styles, but if we are serious about unity we need to share in them.

2.2 Even when strongly aware of unfamiliarity, one can recognise that here are believing Christians who are joining with the whole company of heaven in the offering of worship to God. For many, the Orthodox liturgy conveys powerfully a wonderful sense of the unity of worship offered on earth and in heaven, as well as emphasising the mystery at the heart of the Trinity.

2.3 The largely silent worship of the Religious Society of Friends, where the sense of the presence of God intensifies and where God may speak in the silence to or through individuals, is valued by many in much more 'wordy' Christian traditions.

2.4 The architecture and layout of the buildings and the use of symbols or the deliberate refusal to use them all testify to faith. This means that there is no substitute for encouraging people to worship at the regular services of other churches from time to time, so that each is seen in its usual context. Visitors may realise that it is not 'wrong' to have a crucifix displayed as an aid to devotion. Conversely an empty cross witnesses to the truth of the Resurrection.

2.5 Some of the church buildings may be too small to accommodate the congregations of all the churches on special occasions or at 'united' services. That is a good problem to have! This may mean that the largest building (often the parish church) will be the normal venue of major celebratory worship events.

It is important that this does not reinforce the impression that can easily be given that the Church of England is the natural host for ecumenical events. Some ecumenical worship is deliberately held in secular venues – such as a cinema, or perhaps in a school hall on Education Sunday.

In many places, neighbouring churches are invited to share in the celebration of patronal festivals or services which have a specific focus valued in that tradition.

The Methodist Covenant Service is sometimes celebrated ecumenically – since its value is widely recognised. It should not be used lightly, but at the launch of some piece of ecumenical service or at the end of a time of significant ecumenical sharing, it can be appropriate.

The devotion of the Stations of the Cross, in the Catholic tradition, can be offered in Holy Week to all the churches as can the Renewal of Baptismal Promises.

2.6 Care in explaining the content and flow of the service is always well worth the trouble.

### 3.0 The (Women's) World Day of Prayer

3.1 This is a superb opportunity to experience a sense of the World Church. Material prepared by women representing the Christian churches in a particular country is adapted for use in England, Wales and Ireland (there is a separate Scottish committee).[1] Often there is opportunity for simple dance or drama and the service is usually led entirely by women. On the first Friday of March each year it should be this theme and material that focuses worship in each locality. Try liaising with local schools – perhaps asking them for art work or a dance presentation on the theme.

### 4.0 The Week of Prayer for Christian Unity

4.1 This is an 'Octave' – eight days.[2] In the United Kingdom it is most frequently observed from 18 to 25 January, irrespective of where Sunday falls. Some local Churches Together groupings have deliberately adopted Ascensiontide/Pentecost as the season in which they celebrate the Week of Prayer. It is possible to join in the sense of prayerful expectation conveyed in Acts chapter 1 as the disciples awaited the coming of the Spirit. Some Intermediate Bodies plan a major service during the week somewhere in the county, with church leaders attending and a distinguished preacher.

4.2 In some places there is a feeling of tiredness and predictability about the Week of Prayer. The value of the Week is diminished where there is concentration simply on holding one united service. *"Whose turn is it to host the Week of Prayer Service this year?"* can in some places be the only decision taken, until the last minute. The Week of Prayer leaflet order of service is meant as a basis on which each local group of churches can build its own act of worship – but this needs preparation and rehearsal. The leaflets are designed principally for use by individual Christians in their private devotions, over the eight days.

✳ Some towns have experimented with a corporate meal, followed by worship or with a speaker plus discussion (**Sherborne** and **Bollington**).

* It may be helpful to get away from holding the united service at a time such as Sunday evening which tends to attract smaller numbers anyhow. Many areas are now uniting in their main Sunday **morning** service. This can be viewed as a kind of litmus test of ecumenical commitment! If it is not feasible to have united Sunday worship, the Week of Prayer offers a good opportunity for an exchange of preachers.

* The worship in the Week of Prayer needs to reflect and sum up all that has happened together in the rest of the year, or else it can give the impression *"this is the week when we think about unity"*.

* So often the united service is more a preaching service than a praying service. **Prayer** should be the focal point of worship on this occasion and needs the most careful preparation.

* For the Orthodox the Feast of the Epiphany will fall at the beginning of the January Week of Prayer. Some Orthodox churches have gladly invited fellow Christians to share in the Feast.

## 5.0 **Forms of worship**

5.1 Worship can have many forms even within the one church community. Roman Catholics are not alone in distinguishing between liturgical and non-liturgical worship. Liturgical worship is carried out according to the traditional rites of the church using customs and approved texts, and presided over by an approved worship leader.

5.2 Non-liturgical worship also draws on the common Christian inheritance but can include any appropriate reading, music, or action and can at its best be imaginative, stimulating and participative. This kind of service can be tailor-made to mark a particular occasion or develop a key Christian theme. Many ecumenical services are of this kind. They provide opportunities for individuals or groups attached to one of the churches to offer input. Alternatively, Christians from across the churches can pool their skills in music or drama.[3]

5.3 Many people attest to the value of some symbolic action within such worship – e.g. the sharing of blessed bread (Week of Prayer 1996), weaving together of coloured streamers, making paper chains by writing and linking brief prayers of intercession, attaching prayer 'leaves' to a representative tree or 'flames' to the image of a fire.

5.4 The Taizé Community founded by Brother Roger at the end of World War II specifically to work for reconciliation has developed a style of worship which has a wide ecumenical appeal.[4] Many local Churches Together groupings hold regular Taizé worship as well as encouraging their young people to spend a week or longer at Taizé.

5.5 The Iona Community founded by George McLeod has also offered inspiration to many church traditions.[5] The direct and often poignant Iona lyrics allied to Scottish folk tunes provide a rich source of hymnody for use in ecumenical worship.

5.6 *At Your Service* [6], a publication of the Council of Christian Unity of the

Roman Catholic Bishops' Conference of England & Wales, is an excellent resource for those preparing ecumenical worship. It offers full orders of service for a variety of occasions. There are two separate editions available, each comprising two modest volumes.

5.7 *All Year Round*[7], a loose-leaf quarterly publication of the Council of Churches for Britain & Ireland, is a valuable source of material: mainly prayers and meditations but also hymns, songs and sketches which are suitable for use by groups or at larger celebrations. Where these have been devised for or used at a specific service, the relevant background is given. Material prepared locally which people find particularly helpful or challenging should be submitted for possible inclusion.

5.8 It can be preferable, however, for Christians who want to worship ecumenically to gather and share in the liturgical worship of one of the locally-represented traditions. There has been a definite shift towards this practice. In this way insight can be gained into each other's traditions as well as exposure to the often uncomfortable facts and pain of our disunity. It is not possible to guard against individual Christians taking offence at something within worship practice, but they can and should be encouraged to say what they find objectionable. It may be that they have misunderstood.

---

5.9 **Telford** Christian Council offers the following helpful observation:–

"We have found that if the first steps are in joint worship, we are beginning at the very point of greatest nervousness. However, for example, in *One for the Kingdom* (a service in the Chapel of Christ the King, which follows the patterns of worship of different traditions each month) we have found it possible for Christians from all traditions to share in worship of other forms and then, over coffee, to explore the differences positively and creatively in a non-threatening environment away from their local churches."[8]

---

## 6.0 Eucharistic Worship Together

6.1 It is a profound learning experience to experience the pain of being present at a Eucharistic celebration in which one is prevented by church discipline from receiving bread and wine. Because of their understanding of the nature of the Church, neither Roman Catholic nor Orthodox Churches normally offer eucharistic hospitality to individuals who are not committed to their particular tradition. Nor do they expect their own members to receive the eucharist from celebrants of other traditions. A sensitive explanation of the position should be available well in advance of the service to the members of each church invited, a welcome offered and clear directions given which make the occasion as inclusive as possible.

6.2 It comes as a shock to most people to find out how remarkably similar are our eucharistic liturgies. This, of course, is no accident. Somehow, that makes our inability to offer/accept eucharistic hospitality all the more painful.

> 6.3 "When we came to the Eucharist, I know that, in my heart, I wanted to take Communion, but I am not a member of the Catholic Church, and if I let my heart rule my head then I would cause deep offence. If I remained in my seat, I might equally embarrass my hosts. Evelyn must have read my mind and said "You can go forward to receive a blessing from the priest". As I walked forward, I felt an intense sense of pain, anguish and loss and, as I was blessed, felt very close to my Lord and Saviour. I returned to my seat, knelt down, cried and prayed for my brothers and sisters at St. Mary's. The pain and anguish flowed away, to be replaced by love and peace. I had approached the Lord's table and received of my Lord in the Spirit and I did not walk empty away."[9]

## 7.0 Worshipping together in Holy Week

7.1 Passiontide is a time when devotion to the person of Christ is a priority for most Christians. Many have found that sharing in a Lent programme culminates naturally in united prayer during Holy Week.

> In a suburb of **Newcastle upon Tyne** a series of Meditations on paintings and sculpture was led by one of the industrial chaplains, moving to different churches on different days. Majesty, Perfection, Humanity, Servanthood and Mortality were the themes explored. The Good Friday meditation led into a short procession of witness to the cross outside the shopping centre.

On Maundy Thursday it is usual for Roman Catholic priests to gather at the Cathedral to receive oils for use in baptism, confirmation and anointing in the coming year. Mass that evening in the parishes celebrates the Last Supper and includes the washing of feet and the stripping of the altar in preparation for Good Friday. A vigil is then held until 11-12pm. This means that participation in united eucharists or Passover Meals on Maundy Thursday is difficult. However, other churches could be invited to join in the vigil.

7.2 Palm Sunday and Good Friday are often recognised as days when the churches need to **go public together**. The gospel record of our Lord's triumphal procession into Jerusalem cries out to be celebrated in the open air – much better than trying to bring a donkey into church!

It is extremely difficult to ensure communication between pew and pavement – but it must be attempted. The emphasis should be outward-looking and inclusive. Worship must have 'quality'. Even so, many will feel self-conscious, as though they are "being a fool for the Gospel's sake". Good Friday may also afford an opportunity for a united act of worship and reflection – possibly in the evening.

> 7.3 The **Ilkeston** Association of Christian Churches arranges a Good Friday
> act of worship using four 'stations' – one of them outside. It is one continuous
> service, with a silent walk to the beating of one drum between stations. The
> printed leaflet ends with the following:-
>
> *Our worship continues:*
> *On Easter morning at 6.15 am at Dale Abbey Arch*
> *(in the grounds of Abbey House)*
> *for the Ilkeston Association of Christian Churches Sunrise Service*
> *and*
> *in the churches of the Ilkeston area –*
> *today, tomorrow and Easter Day.*

Every five years there is a bigger Good Friday event enacting the Way of the
Cross from the Entry into Jerusalem to Golgotha.

7.4 Coastal towns often have united worship on the beach on Easter Sunday
morning – sometimes followed by a breakfast picnic. In other places where there
is a prominent local hill, that is selected as an appropriate venue for worship at
dawn. The tradition of some parishes of holding a Resurrection service in the
graveyard on Easter Sunday could be revived as an ecumenical event.[10]

### 8.0 Priority of Praying Together

8.1 The Forum of Churches Together in England in 1995 made this plea:–

"We call on the member churches to encourage us to discover 'the living water'
flowing from God in all denominations. We affirm the need to make **prayer
together** a priority at all levels in our churches. Prayer, theological reflection and
joint action go together."

This led to the setting up of the Churches Co-ordinating Group for Spirituality.

> 8.2 In **Sudbury** the leaders of 13 churches in the area meet monthly for prayer
> in a local convent chapel. There are 15 of them in all – some ordained, some
> not: some paid, some not: some full-time, some not. They represent all
> main-stream traditions. They recognise that praying together undergirds the
> many other initiatives of Churches Together in Sudbury.[11]

8.3 In some localities there is one or more ecumenical prayer group which meets
on a regular basis to pray for unity, peace and local concerns.

8.4 A recent development is of Korean-style early morning prayers (often at 6 or 7
am) held daily or weekly in one of the churches, with people from a variety of
traditions attending regularly. The emphasis is on intercession, but there may be a
brief Bible exposition as well.

8.5 Monthly healing services have become a focus for ecumenical prayer in some places. These may have a particular appeal for those influenced by the charismatic movement. They can also be experienced as divisive if not handled with maturity and sensitivity.

## 9.0 Co-ordinating Intercessory Prayer

9.1 One of the next steps identified in Churches Together in England's Forum 1997's Report to the Enabling Group was to "include in Sunday worship regular intercessions for neighbouring churches and pray for their leaders by name". Many local churches make use of denominational prayer calendars. The World Council of Churches also publishes an Ecumenical Prayer Cycle.[12] It is well worth looking at how these can be supplemented by a leaflet covering local concerns, including prayer for the clergy and people of each local church, local schools, hospitals, hospices and places of employment, with particular days of the week or month allocated to each. It could be used both in Sunday worship in each of the churches and incorporated in prayer material issued for daily private prayer to the members of each congregation. The local newspaper might even be persuaded to carry brief information of this kind on a weekly basis. The interconnectedness of intercession and evangelism is explored in Chapter 10.

9.2 Ecumenical vigils, retreats and prayer groups can all be of value. Vigils have a particular appeal to young people – especially when linked with symbolic action directed to righting injustice, e.g. plight of single homeless, support of asylum seekers.[13]

## 10.0 Styles of prayer and meditation

10.1 There is always more to learn about prayer and how to enrich personal and corporate devotional life. The 1400th anniversary of St. Augustine of Canterbury and St. Columba involved many more people in exploring Celtic spirituality. People of a variety of Christian traditions have gone on Ignatian Individually-Guided Retreats with enormous benefits. Some have developed a form of prayer pilgrimage and prayer walks.[14] A series of United Services or talks developing understanding of different approaches to personal prayer could be a valuable way of exploring the treasures which each church has to offer the others.

-------------------------------------------------------------------------------------

**FOOTNOTES:**

1. World Day of Prayer: Commercial Road, Tunbridge Wells, Kent, TN1 2RR.

2. Week of Prayer for Christian Unity: CCBI Bookshop.

3. See Chapter 15, 6.0 for examples.

4. Taizé: Taizé Community, 71250 Taizé, Cluny, France. Taizé publications are available from CCBI.

5. The Iona Community, The Abbey, Iona, Argyll, PA76 6SN. Wild Goose Publications, Pearce Institute, 840 Govan Road, Glasgow, G51 3UT. (Also available from CCBI).

6. *At Your Service* 1st & 2nd Series. (Available from CCBI).

7. *All Year Round: Uniting in Prayer* (quarterly from CCBI).

8. Telford Christian Council response to *Called To Be One.*

9. Observation and Evaluation Placement for First Year Students, East Midlands Ministerial Training Course, Leslie G. Gill, 1992.

10. Other open-air events are referred to in Chapters 10 and 11.

11. See also Chapter 9, 3.4.

12. *With All God's People: The New Ecumenical Prayer Cycle*, WCC 1990.

13. See Chapter 13, 2.6.

14. See Chapter 10, 5.0.

## 9. CHURCHES LEARNING AND TRAINING TOGETHER

### 1.0 Why Learn Together?

1.1 The churches are becoming aware that learning and Christian nurture happen as least as much through involvement in the life of the Christian community as through formal programmes of instruction. Participating in worship, mutual care and involvement in the work of God in the world forms and shapes Christian disciples and communities.

1.2 There are occasions when learning between, as well as within, churches is appropriate. Hearing one another's stories and experiencing one another's ways of worship, prayer and action will broaden the limited horizons of a particular individual, local church or denomination. New understandings and skills are needed to enable Christians to live and witness effectively in the new Millennium.

1.3 Opportunities should be given to relate to and draw on 'life experience' as well as what some would define more narrowly as 'Christian experience' and to reflect on this together.

1.4 Within the Church everyone has something to offer as well as much to learn. All are teachers and all are disciples. Learning together is for people of every age – adults need opportunity and encouragement as much as if not more than, children and young people. Learning can also be for all ages together – all generations have something to offer each other.

1.5 Christian discipleship is not simply a matter of acquiring information; it is about a relationship with Christ lived out in the body of Christ. Learning which enables **that** must be dynamic and creative.

### 2.0 Examples of what is already happening

2.1 The following illustrate the variety of activities:–

* Adults explore faith together in ecumenical house groups. The use of the CCBI Lent material published for each 'even' year is commended.[1] Training for group leaders is often neglected but increasingly the Intermediate Bodies are providing preparation days for the Lent Course. Detailed suggestions for using or adapting the material are given.

* Churches learn together about their neighbourhood and discover a call to act together in response.

* A joint Holiday Club helps local children to enjoy themselves and to learn together in a Christian context.

* A neighbourhood group of churches holds a day of all age learning activities which leads into worship.

* Shared Sunday School and family worship.

* Adults across the churches explore their faith together and develop their skills for work with children/young people as they use the ecumenically-prepared Kaleidoscope/Spectrum material.[2]
* Two churches considering becoming a Local Ecumenical Partnership (LEP) have a shared church weekend away.
* Participants share a common experience and learning opportunities in an ecumenical pilgrimage to Taizé.
* Young people from across the churches work together on a One World Week theme.

## 3.0 Specific stories and suggestions

### 3.1 Taunton Lent Course

It was found helpful to provide a course tackling meaty theological questions as a formal adult learning experience, run on the initiative of Taunton Churches Together but held at the Further Education College. This raised both the profile and the standard of the course, and attracted between 100 and 200 people each week through Lent.

### 3.2 Cricklade Co-ordination of Joint Worship and Study Groups

Church leaders preached at a series of joint services in Lent. During the week groups met to discuss the sermon, using notes provided by the preachers.

### 3.3 Building Bridges: 1996 CCBI Lent Course

In Croydon each group took seriously the need to apply their findings to the local churches. The group leaders met to see what could be useful to Churches Together in Croydon. This took seriously the criticism that if such study does not result in changes of emphasis in the life of the churches, it can appear self-indulgent.

3.4 The Churches Together in **Sudbury, Suffolk,** have set up Sudbury Christian Youth, which now employs a full-time youth worker. All local ministers took part in his commissioning. The aim was to establish good relationships with the 4,500 young people who come into Sudbury each day to go to school. He takes school assemblies and individual classes in the upper and middle schools. After involvement with a particular young person the youth worker became a member of the local Drugs Action Team, which includes senior schools, police and community representatives. A training scheme for church youth workers has been held and a creative craft club set up. The conversion of a property next door to Gainsborough's house will provide a meeting point for young people. It has been lent rent-free by a local businessman who is currently working abroad but had been praying for such youth work since the mid-1970s.

3.5 **All-age learning** can be fun. 'All Aboard!', the National Christian Education Council's pack for use by activity clubs whether for children or those of all ages is a case in point. Its theme of journeying in faith and life is particularly suited to use in a holiday period.[3]

3.6 **Young people learning together**

The possibility of forming an IMPACT group (under the auspices of the Young Christian Worker Movement) with 14+ age group whether through the secondary school or directly involving young people in the life of the local churches can be looked at.[4] This is primarily a Roman Catholic organisation, but it often operates ecumenically. Issues of living out one's faith are explored, making extensive use of music and drama. Each group has an 'accompanying adult' (often, but not necessarily, a priest or a minister). The 'see-judge-act' method is employed. Personal action on local, national and international justice issues affecting young people is encouraged.

4.0 **Why train together?**

4.1 'Training' is not a word which is often used in local churches, though it is becoming accepted that there are particular Christian ministries (with a small 'm') to which individuals are called, and for which they need and deserve special training. Those with equivalent ministries in different denominations will benefit from being trained together even if there is some part of their role which is specific to their own tradition.

5.0 **Baptism/Confirmation/Membership**

5.1 Most churches expect those seeking baptism for their children to attend some kind of training or preparation. There is an even stronger expectation relating to believer's baptism, confirmation and reception into membership.

5.2 Most of our traditions emphasise that baptism is into the one Church of Christ and that it is by virtue of our common baptism that we recognise each other as fellow Christians. Local churches could consider **together** preparing parents for the baptism of their infants. There are similar opportunities in preparing young people and adults for believer's baptism and confirmation/membership. In view of the significance of joint preparation, examples are given in some detail below.

---

5.3 **Infant Baptism Case Study – St. Basil & All Saints Church Widnes**

At St. Basil & All Saints, which is a Shared Church (Roman Catholic and Church of England), baptism preparation for parents and godparents is conducted by a lay team, mainly of young parents. A locally-drafted three-week course is followed. Week one explores through a short play reasons for seeking baptism; week two uses several short sketches to trace the history of baptism; week three concentrates on explaining the rite and the symbolism used.

---

### 5.4 Believer's Baptism/Confirmation/Membership – Milton Keynes

In **Milton Keynes** an attempt was made to prepare candidates for reception at Easter in line with the Roman Catholic practice of the adult rite of initiation (RCIA). A Confirmation date was fixed with the Anglican bishop very soon after Easter and a "Journey into Faith" group began in the previous October. The various clergy took it in turns to give input at the beginning of the evening, then lay people led discussion groups. The series began by sharing people's experiences of God. Later titles included *"God Comes in Jesus"*, *"The Bible – God's Word"* and *"The Church – God's People"* and before Christmas there was a session on the different traditions represented. After Christmas people went into separate groups. Some time was spent on matters specific to the traditions. It was realised that many other subjects were approached from rather different angles, e.g. sacraments and social teaching, but leaders decided that the time to look at each others' views in these areas was when the candidates were more confident in their own faith. Nearer to Easter, meetings were held on the same evenings but in different rooms, coming together for coffee at the end of the evening.

What had come out of the earlier groups were friendships and an interest in what each other was doing and a desire to go to each other's special services, Anglican/Free Church and Roman Catholic. After the services had taken place the whole group was brought together again to share thoughts and feelings.

### 6.0 Association of Interchurch Families[5]

6.1 This Association has developed immense knowledge and expertise in handling sympathetically the Christian rites of passage. It is encouraging Christian couples who belong to different denominations to maintain and deepen each of their loyalties and to bring up their children in two traditions. It is therefore a source of information and challenge on specific issues. These include:

* the possibilities of infant baptism being celebrated with participation from two churches;
* what is canonically possible when a Roman Catholic marries a person of another denomination;
* under what circumstances the partner may receive communion in the Roman Catholic Church.

The pressure points come at different places depending on the denominational mix – decisions about infant baptism are clearly at their most critical when one partner is firmly convinced that infant baptism is inappropriate.

## 7.0 Churches Together in Marriage[6]

### 7.1 Marriage Preparation - United Christian Parishes of Hedge End[7]

The churches offer two courses a year. A lead couple in the 40-50 year age bracket assisted by a recently-married couple are allocated a group of about six participating couples from a mixture of denominations. Identical letters of invitation, bearing the signature of the young people's own minister, are delivered personally by the group leader who follows this with a telephone call about a week prior to the start of the course.

A brief welcome is given by one of the clergy. A video of 15/20 minutes is then shown and discussed in groups. A leaflet is given out posing thirty questions with a choice of replies from 'him' or 'her'. Participants take the leaflets away to discuss and compare their views and reactions. The evening concludes with coffee.

The course does not attempt to replace doctrinal sessions for those marrying in the Roman Catholic Church and of course there will need to be separate discussion of the detailed arrangements for each marriage service.

7.2 In some localities the need to train marriage counsellors is being explored on an ecumenical basis. *Marriage Encounter* and *Engaged Encounter* initiatives run by Christian lay people deserve to be made more widely known. Marriage Enrichment courses are being taken by couples across the church spectrum.

## 8.0 Bereavement Counselling for Children

8.1 **At Thamesmead LEP** (CofE/Meth/URC/RC) there is a team of trained Christian counsellors who specialise in helping children suffering bereavement. They visit children in their homes and encourage families to talk with their children about the person who has died. Where it is not appropriate to visit, the home counsellors can arrange to talk to children on their own in an attractive room in one of the churches. A network of contacts including schools, health visitors and doctors alerts the centre to children needing help.

## 9.0 Parenting Courses

9.1 Many local churches are responding to the desire for help in parenting, voiced both by people in their own congregation and in the wider community.

### 9.2 *"A Job for Life"* Parenting Skills Project: Ryedale

At the initiative of a trained primary and adult education teacher and marriage counsellor, a Parenting Skills Project using materials from the Family Caring Trust was set up in 1994 with funding for three years. It had the active support of the South Cleveland & North Yorkshire Ecumenical Council and the local Rural Development Commission. Workshops were held in health centres, school halls, church halls and pubs. Further leaders were recruited from among course participants. The course has clearly given people, especially women, new confidence as well as skills. The funding was provided one-third from the churches, one-third from trusts and one-third from the Rural Development Commission. The Management Committee of the Project included representatives of the Anglican and Roman Catholic Dioceses, the Methodist District and the Ryedale Council for Voluntary Action.

## 10.0 Local Preacher/Lay Preacher/Reader Training

10.1 In **Milton Keynes** ecumenical agreement has been reached on a common training course for worship leaders/preachers. This basically follows the Methodist Church nationally approved course *Faith and Worship* but experience is offered in leading worship in Anglican, Baptist, Methodist and United Reformed traditions, recognising that many congregations in Milton Keynes are ecumenical. The qualification is recognised by all participating churches. Each denomination's different history, emphases of worship and ways of ordering church life are dealt with by enabling candidates to grasp and compare both their own and others' ways and histories.

## 11.0 Pastoral Care and Leadership

11.1 The 18 churches comprising **Norwich** Central Churches Together signed a covenant to work, pray, train and evangelise together in 1993. At meetings of representatives since then the themes of training together and sharing faith with others kept surfacing. A working party identified two areas which required particular attention: Pastoral Care and Leadership by lay people in co-operation with clergy, and Mission Outreach. To tackle the first it recommended that the Diocesan Training Team should be asked to conduct their Pastoral Foundation course between Easter 1996 and the end of the year. This involved 16 two-hour sessions, seven in May/June, nine in September/November; cost £24 per student. All this was agreed to. Churches were encouraged to subsidise people where possible. The original working party set up the Pastoral Foundation course starting in May 1996 with two groups involving about 120 people.

## 12.0 Theological and Leadership Training

> 12.1 CONTRAST[8] – Christians of **Nottingham** Training and Studying Together – was set up in 1991 with the active involvement of Churches Together in Nottingham and Churches Together in Nottinghamshire. It includes black and white, both as lecturers/tutors and as students and is available to members of all Christian traditions in the vicinity. In 1995/6 32 students enrolled. At the end of that year three of them went on to further ministerial training. CONTRAST is being integrated into the Certificate programme of the University of Nottingham's Department of Continuing Education. Many students struggle with issues of racial discrimination and class barriers, sharing their own experiences and challenging one another in their search for common ground.

## 13.0 Essential Points to Note

* Specific people need to be asked to explore possibilities and report within a short time scale.
* Training resources do not always have to come from the locality.
* Wider denominational material and expertise should be considered for ecumenical use.
* The churches must be fully informed of the cost involved in adopting a particular programme and work out how this is to be met.
* To advertise and advocate within each local church is absolutely essential.

-------------------------------------------------------------------------------------

## FOOTNOTES:

1. A Lent Course is produced every other year by CCBI.

2. Kaleidoscope: Training Material for those who work with children in the Church, National Christian Education Council (see below).

Spectrum: An inter-church training programme for church youth workers, National Christian Education Council (see below).

3. National Christian Education Council, 1020 Bristol Road, Selly Oak, Birmingham, B29 6NB.

4. Young Christian Workers, 120a West Heath Road, London, NW3 7TY.

5. Association of Interchurch Families, Inter-Church House, 35-41 Lower Marsh, London SE1 7RL. See also Chapter 2, 2.1.

6. A publication of Churches Together in England and CYTUN entitled *Churches Together in Marriage* deals principally with the pastoral care of interchurch marriages but advocates marriage preparation being offered by a local Churches Together grouping.

7. *Family Life Education* Report to Churches Together in England, Helen Lidgett, April 1995.

8. CONTRAST, St. Catherine's House, St. Ann's Well Road, Nottingham, NG3 1EJ.

## 10. CHURCHES EVANGELISING TOGETHER

The variety of ecumenical evangelistic initiatives today demonstrates the potential in going **together** to 'make disciples of every nation'. Evangelising together is not the first, nor the easiest, ecumenical step to take, but the evidence shows it is very worthwhile.

### 1.0 Barriers to Ecumenical Evangelism

1.1 Christians of all denominations are delighted to see new people coming to a living faith in Jesus Christ. Many, however, are cautious of the word 'evangelism'. To some the word conjures up visions of huge set-piece rallies, manipulative tactics and even extreme fundamentalism. In planning any ecumenical evangelistic initiative it is necessary first to talk through the emotional baggage around the word until a common mind is reached – both on the **methods** to be used and on the **nature of the task** to be undertaken. When it is purified of misconceptions, 'evangelism' becomes for many the right word to describe their common task. Others may wish to give it a different label; it is the task that matters, not the word.

1.2 It is important to be as honest and objective as possible as to the underlying reasons for evangelising. If it is because of weakness – falling numbers or financial straits – it will be difficult to come to a mind on the task. Proselytising/sheep-stealing can be a latent (or sometimes dominant) fear. Competitiveness can kill ecumenical evangelism.

1.3 Where understanding and trust are present there can be real joy and delight in working together to reach out to those for whom active involvement in church life and commitment to the Christian faith is a new venture. This kind of confidence cannot be assumed: inter-denominational suspicion is too deeply engrained in our history. It needs to be built – by personal friendships, by wrestling with points of difference, by hearing each others' faith stories/personal testimonies, and by praying together.

### 2.0 Looking at what can realistically be achieved

2.1 It may be helpful to look at what can realistically be achieved. The conversion of someone who has almost no knowledge of the Christian faith to become a devoted follower of Christ rarely happens instantaneously.

The James Engel scale of religious commitment is a useful gauge.

- – 10 Aware of supernatural
- – 9 No effective gospel
- – 8 Initial awareness
- – 7 Interest aroused
- – 6 Basic facts of gospel
- – 5 Implications grasped
- – 4 Positive attitudes
- – 3 Personal need
- – 2 Decision to act
- – 1 Repentance and faith

COMMITMENT
- + 1 Evaluation of Decision
- + 2 Initiation into Church
- + 3 Discipleship – Spiritual Gifts. Witness. Social Action.

Linda Mary Jones, in a study of developing attempts at evangelism in **Bootle**, comments:

"It is only when people are further up the scale that denominational divergences emerge. We need to be realistic and acknowledge the fact that most of the people we meet on our door-to-door visiting and those coming for the occasional offices are at the –10 level. It is a long process to get someone from –10 to –1. If we can work together to interest people in the Gospel that we share then we can go on to nurture that interest and allow each denomination to bring people to a decision in a denomination and style of worship that they feel comfortable in.

Most evangelism aims at the people in the –3 to +3 range. *Living Faith in the City* says that mass evangelism is not effective in urban areas, because so many have no contact with the church or the Christian faith."[1]

2.2 John Finney's survey of how adults come to faith *Finding Faith Today*[2] stresses the importance of personal relationships in evangelism and the length of time it takes for most people to find faith and make a public commitment to Christ within a local congregation. This needs to be understood by the local churches.

### 3.0 Training in Evangelism

3.1 Many Christians lack confidence in evangelism because they are unsure about what is distinctive in their own faith and are cautious about going out with a level of 'boldness' which is difficult to square with the many questions they are still struggling with. The **Alpha Course**[3] is valued as a training tool by a wide range of Christians. It is being used ecumenically especially in villages and small towns. Its value is attested both as a tool for confidence-building among existing members and in attracting and challenging non-Christians. Trust and loving relationships will be built up.

3.2 The Bible Society's **Church Growth**[4] course has been conducted for a number of local councils of churches or Churches Together groupings – either over a weekend or a series of evenings. **Norwich Central Churches Together** has embarked on this and has also asked a working group to make recommendations on how lay people can be encouraged and helped to "gossip the gospel". There is evidence that women are more likely to influence their friends/partners to become Christians than are men. Individuals need to be affirmed in what they can do, and encouraged to have non-Christian friends and interests that extend beyond the church.

## 4.0 Evangelising Possibilities

4.1 All evangelistic activity requires thorough planning. There are many possibilities and a growing number of opportunities.

4.2 Evangelising **new areas** opens up exciting possibilities. In some places major housing development is planned and a local Churches Together grouping needs to be ready to offer the gospel not only in providing opportunities for worship but in helping to build community.[5] Above all the churches must avoid operating competitively. In some places it has been possible to appoint an evangelist financially supported by and responsible to the local Churches Together grouping.

4.3 Presence has been found to be a pre-requisite for evangelism. Especially where housing development is still in progress it is vital that church workers live **in** the area and identify with it. There are various nationally operated schemes which offer **young volunteers** to work for pocket money for six months or a year in a church-based project.

In **Abbey Meads, Swindon**, while it was still a building site the Methodist deaconess was at work on behalf of Churches Together. The Local Ecumenical Partnership there was inaugurated on a lorry!

4.4 There are numerous examples of church groupings adopting the well-tried format of using a **major ecumenical mission**. Those coming to faith are referred to local churches who follow them up. This is not an easy or cheap option for local churches, who need to have a long run-in period, ensuring that they are adequately prepared, have mobilised their people in prayer, have secured appropriate publicity, are committed as individuals to inviting non-Christian friends, have trained counsellors and have basic Christian teaching programmes in place to offer to serious enquirers.

4.5 **Festival '92** in **Leeds** demonstrated that a limited, defined aim of raising the profile of the churches and the gospel can be of value. It worked for a five-fold impact: Prayer, Presence, Proclamation, Persuasion, Power and encouraged local church groupings to arrange events in their locality. These proved more successful than major central events.

4.6 **'Wakefield Awake'** in 1994 held over 100 events during two weeks and left people in the city in no doubt that the church is alive and well. It aimed to show how much the church had to offer the people of the city. Events included an evening with Adrian and Bridget Plass, performances of Haydn's *"Creation"* and the musical *Alpha & Omega*, a presentation of the OASIS Video Road Show, a Children's Day at the Cathedral and several art exhibitions. 40,000 copies of a directory of local churches were delivered to homes in the city with a personal greeting from local churches by couples representing two different traditions.

4.7 In **Leicester** a team of 80 students associated with St. Aldate's Church Oxford was invited to lead an evangelical mission over a period of 10 days. It involved other evangelical fellowship groups as well as members of the local council of churches, and was found to have a unifying effect. The sense of competition was at a minimum. Outsiders were able to operate in more uninhibited ways than local people could. They were also able to train and empower those already in the church.

4.8 The *One Voice* ecumenical evangelism initiative in **Wallasey** did not gain the confidence of most of the laity, perhaps because they were not offered adequate training. People were reluctant to go to an event in a church with which they did not identify. The barn dance was a huge success, though! The children's 'Big Bin' event worked well and is still running. The ecumenical Prayer Group which began to undergird the venture is still meeting every Friday.

4.9 **The Humberside Festival of Faith** in June 1995 has been one of the most ambitious , covering the whole of the former County of Humberside. Under the county-wide umbrella, local events included open days, Songs of Praise, open air services, street theatre, praise & prayer on ice and public bible reading from Hull City Hall Balcony.

4.10 **Special Events** arranged by Churches Together groups in different places have included *On Fire*, a Pentecost act of witness, youth nights with special speakers, a two-year programme of events, and events led by the Church of England's Springboard Team but organised ecumenically. It is well worth local groupings of Churches Together 'buying' into wider celebrations.

It is important to find a suitable time of year for a special event. *Making Waves* in **Plymouth** made less impact than it might have done because it co-incided with a major holiday period.

4.11 **Churches Together in Dronfield**: 1994 was designated 'The Year of Living Hope.' Member churches organised and advertised a co-ordinated Mission, making sure that each other's events did not clash. The churches only felt able to embark on this after working closely together for many years. The development of a thoroughgoing network of pastoral care on a street-by-street basis had given them credibility in the town (see Chapter 11,4.1). In August there were successive weeks of children's club activities hosted by different churches to build up Sunday School and youth work. House-to-house joint visitation took place in September and a joint mission to the secondary school. During the autumn each denomination had its own distinct week of mission. It was recognised that in the end individuals need to link up with a particular worshipping congregation.

4.12 **"Abingdon Alive" Festival** held over 30 events in a two week period, culminating at Pentecost in a celebration linked to *On Fire*.

4.13 **Ridley Market Open Air Evangelism**: Evangelistic events are held in the open air at this market in **Hackney** on most Saturdays when churches take it in turn to lead in a style they are happy with.

4.14 **The Open House Coffee Shop**: an ecumenically-run cafe in a suburb of **Sheffield** with bookshop, free literature, listening and prayer counselling available on request is a long-term project. It has run an Alpha Course.

4.15 Churches Together in **Wickersley** in South Yorkshire has held an annual outreach festival each October since 1991 with a shared prayer vigil, a shared main event with speakers that is followed by a series of smaller events in each of the churches, and shared publicity for the follow-on invitation to any who are interested in exploring the Christian faith. Each church then holds a 'basics course' for enquirers. This amounts to shared evangelisation, with mutual respect for each church's own identity.

## 5.0 Marches of Witness (e.g. Good Friday)/March for Jesus/Prayer Walks

5.1 Christians take to the streets to witness, pray and sing. Combined with attractive leaflets this can be a useful piece of occasional evangelism.

In **South Shields** each church lined up behind its own banner for the March for Jesus. Many found this a source of embarrassment which led to a point of repentance: "What right have we to proclaim a gospel which speaks of reconciliation when we are divided?" There was no place for triumphalism or rivalry. The following year there was ready agreement that church banners would not feature. Instead banners were made showing symbols of Pentecost.

5.2 Many would agree that a March of Witness should be first and foremost an act of worship made more accessible to non-churchgoers by not requiring them to come through church doors. While some churches speak naturally of "spiritual warfare", others find any military connotations worrying, so that the very idea of 'marching' may be repugnant. Awareness of the use of marching to strengthen religious 'tribal' loyalties in Northern Ireland may also make it inappropriate. In multi-cultural neighbourhoods the sight of people coming in numbers down their street bearing Christian symbols may evoke fears of Crusades and Holy Wars.

5.3 An alternative to a March can be a **Prayer Walk**.

---

In an initiative '**Time for Barnsley**' several hundred Christians between them walked round the 75 mile perimeter of the borough on a Saturday in May 1997. Simultaneous prayer took place at agreed times at different points on the boundary. At mid-day the walkers were joined in prayer by many others, less mobile, meeting in their local churches. An evening Prayer Concert followed, led by Graham Kendrick, at the Oakwell football ground. There over 1,500 prayed again for the Barnsley community, for measures being taken to tackle unemployment, for regeneration of urban priority areas, for family life, for the police and the courts and those in fear of crime and violence. 107 of the 139 churches in the borough were involved in some way, a remarkable achievement in a town with little history of the churches working together. The event took three years to plan and is being followed up by launching neighbourhood 'watch and pray' schemes for particular areas.

---

## 6.0 House-to-House Visitation

6.1 There is still a place for systematic house-to-house visitation, especially when carried out ecumenically, leaving simple literature with service times and telephone numbers of clergy.

---

In **Bootle** a joint Anglican/Roman Catholic programme was arranged. (Baptists and Salvation Army who drew their congregations from a wider area did not feel able to join in.) 'The St. Monica's people were taken aback that we were not just talking about visiting but were actually going to do it. They were excited about beginning, though terrified.' Visiting was planned to take place every Tuesday evening during British Summer Time, preceded by brief prayer and followed by prayer and fellowship, thus reinforcing the sense of all being in this together under God.

---

The story below illustrates that there may be a long time lag in response:

'One of the recent St. Matthew's confirmation candidates had come into the church through the door-to-door visiting. She had been visited back in 1990. The vicar went back some months later and because the person was out he left a card.

Several months later she rang up for the times of services and started coming. At the party after the confirmation she said "You hadn't forgotten me. I still have the card you put through my door. I wasn't ready to come then but when I was I knew you would remember me."[6]

6.2 Systematic visiting offering to pray for people's concerns has proved its worth.

> In **Hutton Rudby** a letter was sent to every house in a given area in the village, explaining that the three churches of the village would be praying for that area and that someone would call to ask if there were any requests people would like taken back to the churches on the following Sunday. Members of the churches then go out in twos, always representing different churches. The report back was "The results have both surprised and moved us. Nowhere have we met with any unpleasantness. Only 10% said they were not interested; 40% said they thought it was a good idea but had not particular requests; about half had something they wanted us to pray for ..... A further round of visits produced a higher proportion of requests, and some very moving experiences where people trusted us with their problems and their joys." A few people went to church specifically to join in as prayers were offered for them. Those involved in the visiting speak of how strengthened and uplifted they were by the experience and how widespread seems to be the belief in the power of prayer. All the churches observe the requests for prayer in their Sunday worship.[7]

## 7.0 Christian Enquiry Agency[8]

7.1 The Christian Enquiry Agency engages in billboard, newspaper, handbill and beer-mat low-key advertising: respondents contact the Agency for literature and, if desired, referral to local churches. It has been demonstrated that this has an appeal to young men – the section of the population that most churches find it hardest to involve. Simple material inviting further enquiry could be made available for mourners at the local crematorium. It is a fine line between abusing individuals by exerting undue pressure at a time of heightened emotion, and losing an opportunity to help them reflect on the large 'why?' questions of life and death. This is an area where churches could well work out a policy together.

## 8.0 Churches Group for Evangelisation[9]

8.1 The member churches of Churches Together in England have a Group for Evangelisation, which includes also some members of the Evangelical Alliance, thus providing a link with churches which have not traditionally been part of main-stream ecumenism.

## 9.0 Conclusion

9.1 Can churches evangelise together? Yes, if they are willing to do the groundwork and surmount the barriers. As with all ecumenical ventures, it is more work in the short term to do it together than separately, but it has great potential. The dividedness of the Christian Church has long been a barrier to faith for many: a joint Christian outreach to unchurched people is a healthy corrective which can draw many into the kingdom of God.

-----------------------------------------------------------------------------------------------------

## FOOTNOTES:

1. Archbishops' Diploma for Readers Submission 1993. Linda Mary Jones.

2. *Finding Faith Today*, John Finney, 1992, Bible Society.

3. Alpha Course: for details write to Holy Trinity Church, Brompton Road, London SW7 1JA.

4. Bible Society: Stonehill Green, Westlea, Swindon, Wiltshire, SN5 7DG.

5. See Chapters 11 and 12.

6. See Note 1 above.

7. *Pilgrim Post*, January 1995.

8. Christian Enquiry Agency, Inter-Church House, 35-41 Lower Marsh, London SE1 7RL. Tel: 0171 620 4444.

For contact names of those involved in specific evangelistic events referred to in this Chapter, write to Churches Together in England (North & Midlands) Office.

9. Churches Group for Evangelisation, c/o Inter-Church House.

# LIVING AND WORSHIPPING TOGETHER

## 11. CHURCHES SERVING THEIR LOCALITY TOGETHER

### 1.0 Faith into Action

1.1 The 1987 Swanwick Declaration spoke of "common evangelism and service of the world" as an essential part of the search for unity in God's world". In 1997 Churches Together in England Forum endorsed "responding to human need by loving service" as one of the marks of mission. Personal and corporate evangelism must be an essential part of every church's life and action, but that should not exhaust our commitment to serve the whole of God's creation – his *oikoumene.*

1.2 Reflecting mainly the American scene, Jim Wallis writes:

"After years of very limited results from institutional ecumenical dialogues, a vital ecumenism is emerging between people who have found one another while putting their faith into action."[1]

1.3 Churches which serve the same community – be that village, town, housing estate, or inner city – have the basis for their work on their own immediate doorstep. This is the place for common witness and service. The deepest relationship between churches of varying traditions and spirituality is often found when they put their faith into action in their own community. This can be the cement which makes ecumenism effective and real.

### 2.0 Building Community

2.1 All our human communities are suffering from a lack of cohesion because of greater mobility, breakdown of family life, and disillusionment with political and civic life. Where churches see their mission together in the locality they not only create their own small Christian communities, but go some way to creating a better and more Christian community for everyone. The Christian witness of individuals and churches is urgently needed in every community today.[2]

### 3.0 Service Together

3.1 Practical examples abound where churches have the vision of united mission in word and deed. Statutory bodies in civic, education, social service and medical fields welcome the opportunity to work with a Churches Together structure whether that it is city-wide or the informal arrangements in a village. Sadly it still seems that the bench mark of so much local ecumenical work is 'joint services' rather than 'joint service'.

3.2 Local authorities are usually happy to work with churches in Christian Neighbourhood schemes, luncheon clubs, bereavement visiting and many other fields of joint concern. Such co-operation can earn the churches the opportunity to say why they are doing these everyday things together for the total community. Increasingly churches are seeing Christian service as an essential part of the gospel, but so much more can be done when all the churches in a locality pool their resources of buildings, people and contacts. It is good when folk say "see how these Christians love one another" – it is even better when they can say "see how these Christians love everyone"!

## 4.0 Examples:

---

### 4.1 Road Steward Scheme, Dronfield

The 14 churches of Churches Together in **Dronfield & District** set up a Road Steward scheme in conjunction with the Town Council, and 400 members were recruited and trained to work on behalf of the local authority and the churches. The Town Council provide 250 copies of the town guide each year, and these are then included in a brochure with the local church magazine and other material, and given to all newcomers as they move in. The Road Stewards also give a personal welcome to newcomers and thereafter act as a link with the churches and keep them in touch with those who are ill or in trouble of any sort. This scheme has been running for seven years and is working well. No one church could give the 90% coverage which is achieved throughout the community of 27,000 in the town and surrounding villages.

---

### 4.2 CHIN – Christian Helpline in Newlyn

**Newlyn** is a fishing village in the far west of Cornwall, situated between Penzance and Mousehole. There are Methodist chapels, one Anglican church and a Mission for Fishermen. In 1985 when the Government announced its Social Services Review, it was felt that it would adversely affect those in greatest need. The Newlyn Methodist Community Group was formed in July 1985. Members of the St. Peter's Anglican Church joined with them in December 1986. The ecumenical group became CHIN, Christian Helpline in Newlyn. Having begun with six volunteers, by 1995 there were 102 from 10 churches in the area. The volunteers answer the telephone, provide essential transport to hospitals, surgeries, day centres, etc., give practical help and befriending. Trained counselling is available. Volunteers are vetted, references taken up and all carry an identity card. CHIN supports carers and one-parent families, also many anxious and depressed clients, who need someone to talk to. During 1994/5 695 calls were received. Approximately half of these came from people needing help, their families or friends and the remainder came from professional bodies with whom there are strong links. Supporters of CHIN meet to pray together on the first Monday of each month.

---

### 4.3 Joint meetings

Many churches have a branch of an organisation dedicated to practical service, e.g. Knights of St.Columba (Roman Catholic) and League of the Good Samaritan (Free Church). These could well have some joint meetings and share expertise and knowledge of the needs of the community.

In **Petworth**, Churches Together Befrienders is a wider group developed from St. Vincent de Paul Society, involving Anglicans, Catholics, United Reformed and the Evangelical Church in the village. They have advertised their availability by means of a card delivered to each household, headed "Friendship without Strings".

## 4.4 Alcohol-free Bar

The incidence of vandalism or the complaint of teenagers that "there's nothing to do and nowhere to go" may galvanise local churches into some 'unattached' youth provision. Often a basic place to meet, with an **alcohol-free bar** is the main requirement. If this is not on church premises, it will have a wider appeal. It does need a reliable team of adults who can empathise with young people. Many will need training. *Safe from Harm* Guidelines must be followed.[3]

One example is the Carpenter's Arms, **North Walsham**, where the bar is managed by two part-time managers and a group of 30 volunteers. The need for additional bar space, facilities for counselling and for recreational activities have already become evident. The project is supported by Churches Together in North Walsham.

## 4.5 South Bristol Youth Bus

In **South Bristol**, in common with many other areas, problems had been experienced with young people vandalising and causing trouble in shopping precincts, stealing, taking drugs and generally being out of control. In 1991 the George Muller Foundation was invited by concerned clergy to help them provide a Youth Bus in Bristol South, to be maintained, run and financed by the churches. Over a dozen congregations pooled their skills, resources and energy to provide the bus which caters for 11-14 year olds, in a different area of the city each evening, and staffed by the local churches. Many of the young people have come regularly over a period of years and are now being given help and encouragement as they seek appropriate training and job opportunities. The Project would not have been possible for any of the churches on its own.

## 4.6 Winsford Child Contact Centre

At the request of local magistrates in Winsford, Cheshire, the local churches together grouping has set up a child contact centre, staffed ecumenically, providing neutral ground on which separated/divorced parents can have access to their children. The children are the responsibility of the parent or other relative whilst at the centre but volunteers keep a register, 'guard' the exit, make tea, chat to anyone who is bored or distressed and try to ensure that the children are having a positive experience of contact. This is self-evidently a very valuable service to offer.[4]

### 4.7 Community Development in Malvern

Following a presentation on local deprivation, **Malvern Churches Community Network** was initiated by Churches Together in Malvern. Together with the Diocesan Board for Social Responsibility it provided the funds to employ a community development worker who has since been able to attract grants to fund a variety of projects. These include an after-school/holiday Kids' Club, a toy library, a clothing store and an electrical goods recycling scheme. The Network works closely with local social services, a housing association, police and Community Action, the local volunteer organisation.

### 4.8 Egremont 'CAFE'

Churches may step in to maintain a level of service which is threatened. In **Egremont**, Cumbria, Community Action for Egremont (with the acronym CAFE) was established in September 1995 as a self-help group when the official Job Centre was closed. Arrangements were made to relay job vacancies from the nearest Centre at Cleator Moor and to continue to provide in Egremont information on training and benefits. Since then a Community Law Centre has also been set up, holding a weekly surgery. The possibility of setting up a Credit Union is also being explored. A longer-term aim is to establish an Enterprise Centre from which community businesses could operate. Community Action for Egremont is a partnership of the local Churches Together (Anglican, Methodist and Roman Catholic), Copeland Borough Council and Egremont Town Council. The Centre is open from 1 pm to 4 pm from Monday to Friday.

### 4.9 Jarrow Credit Union

The North-East is a particularly fertile ground for Credit Unions and many of these have been formed at the instigation of Churches Together groupings. **Jarrow** is a case in point. A Credit Union encourages regular modest saving and enhances the local economy as money is always lent to local members for provident or productive purposes. A Credit Union requires a team of 11 people to run it and a nine/twelve month basic training is available. Because of the pressures to purchase major household items **now** – "no deposit – no repayments for six months" – many families are deep in debt. Churches may also be involved in setting up Debt Counselling Services. This could be an appropriate local response of the churches at the same time as they campaign for the remission of Third World Debt through Jubilee 2000.

## 4.10 Leighton Buzzard Youth Training Scheme

Some projects which rely heavily on external funding will be especially vulnerable to changes of government policy. An example is **Leighton Buzzard**, where a major Churches Together sponsored Youth Training Scheme worked for a number of years with youngsters with poor social skills and low educational achievement. It evolved successfully into a limited company, but at the point where funding became dependent on qualifications achieved, there was no option but to close down. This proved a painful decision and process. It was only afterwards that some at least of those most heavily involved were able to recognise that there had been more than 10 years of solid achievement and that many people's lives had been given a measure of dignity and purpose. Some people felt that the churches had been 'used' – others accepted that following Christ's way of sacrificial service may lead to the cross.

Through Christian history churches have often pioneered responses to community need. If these are later adapted or taken over by other agencies, this does not mean that the church action was inappropriate. Nor does it mean that churches have to hold on to the reins of everything that they initiate.

---

**FOOTNOTES:**

1. *Soul of Politics*, Jim Wallis, p.46.

2. Churches Community Work Alliance (a Co-ordinating Group of Churches Together in England), 36 Sandygate, Wath-upon-Dearne, Rotherham, S63 7LW, provides practical support for projects and contributes to churches' thinking on mission in community work.

3. See Chapter 6, 7.

4. Network of Access and Child Contact Centres, St. Andrew's with Castlegate URC, Goldsmith Street, Nottingham, NG1 5JT. Tel/Fax: 0155 948 4557.

## 12. CHURCHES RELATING TO THEIR LOCAL AUTHORITY TOGETHER

### 1.0 Appropriate geography

1.1 While it is in neighbourhoods that ecumenism comes alive for most people, some tasks can more appropriately be done in a wider geography. Civic consciousness varies widely in intensity from place to place and even within any one town. The city centre churches (including cathedrals) may have a special role in focusing this and may well be appropriate venues for meetings to air civic issues. The danger that only the city centre churches get involved in relating to the local authority is a real one – hence the argument for the city-wide or unitary authority-wide Churches Together grouping. Similarly, in a Churches Together group which serves a small town and its surrounding district, town concerns can tend to dominate. Some rural issues can be handled locally: often the county ecumenical body will be seeking to address these but will rely on more local knowledge and action.

### 2.0 The Local Authority standpoint

2.1 A major justification for forming a Churches Together grouping at the level of a sizeable town or city is to provide a mechanism for relating to the local authority. If this is not done, either there will be no consultation with the churches, or the consultation will tend to be only with the Church of England. Increasingly, local authorities are expected to liaise with other statutory bodies, and with health, education, voluntary and commercial bodies.

2.2 Central government and local authority provision is being reduced and other bodies are being expected to make 'bids' to meet needs which only a few years ago were clearly seen as the responsibility of statutory bodies. 'Partnership' is in vogue and provides new opportunities for the churches to play a significant part in the community.

2.3 The Bishop of Southwell responded to the prospect of Single Regeneration Budget funding in inner city **Nottingham** in an imaginative way by seconding one of his senior clergy to represent the churches as part of the voluntary sector input. The person seconded worked with the Programmes and Strategies office of the Chief Executive to increase the involvement of Christian and Inter-Faith networks across the city in regeneration initiatives. The four-month experiment was followed up by a second secondment of another inner city vicar for the next four months. This was an Anglican initiative with thoroughly ecumenical aims. The ability to move quickly when operating to meet government/European Community deadlines may often need to take precedence over desirable ecumenical consultation.

## 3.0 Co-operative way of working

3.1 Churches can either wring their hands on the sidelines or seek to be alongside other players in tackling a range of issues close to the heart of their concern. The latter can be termed the CO-OPERATIVE way of working. In some places chaplaincy is provided to the local authority itself (e.g. **Cleveland** County Council until its demise), to the fire service and the police. The expectation must be that councillors are working for the good of the community. The churches should beware of getting caught up in prevalent cynicism of the role and motives of locally elected members. However, it is also important to avoid being used for party political ends.

---

3.2 When the new **North-East Lincolnshire** Unitary Authority was planned the Churches Together groups in Grimsby and Cleethorpes both recognised the need to form links with the new authority. During 1995 the Bishop of Grimsby was invited to address both groups and a consultation with representatives of the new Authority was requested as a result. An exploratory meeting on joint working between the churches and the local authority was held on 2 April 1996, only the second day of its existence! This was a very open and fruitful meeting. It was followed by a mutual presentation to the unitary authority in the autumn at which the churches shared some of their work and concerns and the authority offered presentations on some of its key work to the church representatives. A pattern of regular meetings has been established.

---

3.3 Many kinds of social provision now rely on an expectation of a professional level of care by voluntary bodies.

---

The **Sheffield** Churches Council for Community Care originally pioneered Good Neighbour Schemes, diversified into Hospital After Care, a Bereavement Support Scheme and an Escort Care service. Major funding comes from the local authority, the hospitals and local trusts as well as the churches.

---

In a much smaller place, the local Churches Together group through **Wickersley** Neighbourhood Group (WING) provides a drop-in centre for the elderly and a street warden scheme in close consultation with Rotherham Metropolitan Borough Council.

---

(Many of the pieces of work illustrated in other chapters involve close co-operation with and sometimes ongoing funding from the local authority.)[1]

## 4.0 Critical way of working

4.1 There is also a CRITICAL way of working. Such bodies as **The Gospel as Public Truth** and **Christians in Public Life** are challenging the churches to enable their members to make judgements on when to co-operate with and when to stand out against decisions of national and local bodies. Advocacy on behalf of the marginalised and victims of injustice remains a prime duty of the churches who should beware of being compromised by partnership with the powerful. Particular denominations may well come down at different points on a co-operative – critical continuum. Not all churches are prepared to bid for national lottery funds, for example.

4.2 Circumstances may necessitate a Churches Together grouping acting in co-operation with the authorities on some occasions while distancing itself at other times. Certain local churches may on grounds of conscience and church teaching feel bound to oppose specific government or local government policies. If they identify strongly with their area, they may all too readily tend to resist all major new proposals, e.g. new housing estates, provision for travellers, secure hostels, which can be perceived as altering the character of the area. The ability of local churches to minister to the needs of particular groups in society or to future residents can be jeopardised if the churches adopt a strong 'political' stance.

4.3 A new movement originating in the United States is beginning to make itself felt in the major conurbations of England. It is known as **Broadbased Organising**.[2] Six such organisations were in operatation in 1996 in the UK, and is concerned with re-establishing the principle of accountable relationships in public life. To get all sorts of people talking, arguing, agreeing and developing trust between themselves is seen as the way to build safe, vibrant and healthy communities. Through travelling to see such operations elsewhere people have come back highly motivated to fulfil their Christian call to service. Others, who have undergone specific training, have discovered a new sense of their own worth and a capacity to support and promote common action. A Roman Catholic parish gives this verdict: "The parish has begun through Broadbased Organising activity to find a way to translate their faith into deeds which are potentially life-giving and life-enhancing." There is a clear appeal to those with a concern for social justice who are frustrated by traditional party political representation. Broadbased Organising can bring together very diverse groups – Christian, Muslim, Sikh, Hindu, rich and poor, black and white, young and old and from very different political allegiances. It is clearly an excellent way of building inter-faith relationships and bridges.

## 5.0 Functions Appropriate to Umbrella/Wider Groupings

The following functions can be identified but are not necessarily exhaustive:–

5.1 Clarifying the **relationship** of the umbrella body to local Churches Together groups within its catchment area and establishing and maintaining good **communication**. A **directory** of local churches and clergy–contact people within the local authority area (updated annually) can be produced by someone other than the Churches Together secretary, and should be made widely available to public libraries, Citizens' Advice Bureaux etc.

> *The Churches' Directory of Churches, the Local Authority and Voluntary Organisations in the Borough of Croydon* has been produced annually for 27 years. It makes no distinction between those local churches which are members of Churches Together in **Croydon** and those which are not, but seeks to provide comprehensive information.

5.2 Arranging **introduction to Xtown days** for new clergy and ministers. In **Sheffield**, for example, a day of this kind is held each September.

5.3 Circularising the churches with a list of **local councillors** and the times of their regular surgeries for displaying on church notice boards.

5.4 Arranging regular **meetings of church leaders with MPs** or local councillors.

> This is a strong feature in **Birmingham** – a place where civic pride has long relied on close relationships with leaders of Christian churches. This relationship is now being developed with other faith communities as well.

5.5 Securing the appointment of **Borough Deans**.

> In the **London Boroughs** each of the major denominations appoints a senior priest or minister to be the contact for that denomination with the Local Authority. These Borough Deans should be among the representatives on an umbrella Churches Together body.

5.6 Being a party to an agreed strategy and procedure for **responding to major disasters.** This may be handled at a city-wide or a county-wide level.

5.7 Ensuring that the **Planning Authority** advise the Churches Together secretary of major proposals for housing/employment/redevelopment so that the churches may have the opportunity to co-ordinate their strategy. This will include the opportunity to be represented in funding bids, e.g. Single Regeneration Budget or European Funding.

5.8 Arranging **pre-election meetings** where parliamentary candidates can be questioned on party policy. The Council of Churches for Britain and Ireland provides guidelines for such events. Church Action on Poverty and other agencies suggest key questions to put to candidates.[3]

5.9 Securing the **appointment** of appropriate church representatives to a variety of committees and working groups, e.g. education, race relations.

5.10 Hosting **debates or day conferences on topics with important ethical dimensions** that have particular relevance to the town/city.

5.11 Arranging training days for those serving as **school governors** – a very demanding commitment.

5.12 **Inter-faith linking** at a town or city-wide level.

5.13 Co-ordination of church involvement in **town-twinning schemes.**[4]

6.0 **Boundaries**

6.1 The city-wide Churches Together grouping assumes particular importance where there is major new planned population growth which cuts across existing ecclesiastical or civil boundaries.

---
In both **Telford** and **Milton Keynes** – major new towns – the fact that the churches have been able to operate in a thoroughly ecumenical way has enabled remarkable co-operation with first the Development Corporation and latterly the local authority. Mutual respect has resulted.
---

7.0 **Constitutional Considerations for a Local Authority-wide Churches Together Grouping**

7.1 Appendix III(a) suggests helpful questions to ask when exploring different options.

Appendix III(b) sets out a model constitution for an umbrella body.

7.2 The precise role of such umbrella bodies is still being explored. There is a lot of misunderstanding and sometimes excessive claims are made. Some cities have in despair abolished their overall Council of Churches, recognising that most people relate more readily to their locality. However, soon after abolition the need for some co-ordination often becomes apparent.

---
**Northampton** is a case in point. A few years after the borough-wide Council of Churches was scrapped, a new umbrella body was formed. In May 1997 Churches Together in Northampton & District was launched at a united service attended by the Mayor of Northampton, a Sikh.
---

Where there is a Free Church Council serving the town or city, it is desirable to incorporate its functions within the umbrella Churches Together. This can be done by providing for a Free Church Committee which can meet to decide matters of specific Free Church concern.[5]

## 8.0 Summary

8.1 The churches are spurred to action in a variety of ways. Cases of local hardship which need a pastoral response may lead to the Churches Together groupings forming alliances with agencies with a very specific or much wider brief. Often the challenge to the churches will come from an outside agency. The Churches Together grouping should be prepared to work with both statutory and non-statutory bodies. There is no virtue in even the Churches Together doing it alone. Remember the Corby Principle![6]

-------------------------------------------------------------------------------------

## FOOTNOTES:

1. See, for example, Chapters 9 4.7 and 13 3.6.

2. Broadbased Organising, Citizen Organising Foundation, 200 Bunbury Road, Northfield, Birmingham, B31 2DL.

3. Church Action on Poverty: Central Buildings, Oldham Street, Manchester, M1 1JT.

4. See Chapter 14, 5.0.

5. See Appendix III (b) Note 9.

6. See Chapter 1, 2.3.

## 13. CHURCHES ADDRESSING JUSTICE, PEACE AN ENVIRONMENTAL ISSUES TOGETHER

### 1.0 The churches' calling to be agents of reconciliation

1.1 Both stories of creation in Genesis (Gen 1.1 – 2.3 & 2.4 – 25) present a world in which there is unity with God and with itself. This original unity is broken and there then follows the unfolding of salvation as the restoration of that unity. God becomes human as an act of love to restore all creation to its original state of unity – enabling people to live in an intimate relationship with God, with other human beings and with the whole of creation.

1.2 In this divided world, all are called by God to be reconciled to each other; to bring reconciliation to those who are in need both of justice and peace as well as caring for all of God's creation. The last two of the five marks of mission[1] highlighted at the CTE Forum 1997 make this clear –

*seeking to transform unjust structures of society* and

*striving to safeguard the integrity of creation, sustaining and renewing the life of the earth.*

1.3 **Justice:** Millions of people lack basic necessities of life; in poor countries people die and even in rich countries many live in poverty. The debt crisis is a major economic injustice. Human rights are being violated on a huge scale.

**Peace:** Over 100 wars have been fought since 1945. Massive arsenals of nuclear and other weapons threaten the human race. World-wide arms spending consumes vast resources.

**Integrity of Creation:** It is vital to live in equilibrium with all of God's creation. Thousands of animal and plant species have become extinct. Industrial and agricultural technologies and energy consumption damage ecology, causing greenhouse effect and damaging the ozone layer. Trees die, waters are poisoned and polluted.

1.4 Local Churches Together groups can share their vision of *shalom* (Hebrew word for peace with prosperity) which leads us to become involved in the struggle with all those who share our vision in the struggles against injustice and all that is life-threatening. It is possible to work together for a just, participatory and sustainable society.

1.5 Members of Churches Together need to examine their own lifestyles to see if they are consistent with the Justice, Peace and Integrity of Creation that God requires. Start with a topical or common local issue and listen for God's call to respond to it. There are so many issues. Guard against attempting to address too many at one time. Discussion that is set in a context of prayer and Bible study is likely to prove most helpful.

1.6 National initiatives will often suggest themes for local action, e.g. Christian Aid Week (mid-May), Racial Justice Sunday (2nd Sunday in September), One World Week (mid-October), Prisoners' Week (mid-November).

1.7 Young people are particularly concerned about the issues addressed in this chapter. See also Churches Learning & Training Together (Chapter 9, 3.6). Moreover, it is unlikely that many young people will be interested in local ecumenism unless these issues are addressed.

## 2.0 Some ecumenical responses on issues of Justice

2.1 **Jubilee 2000**[2]: Throughout the country local churches have been challenged to sign a petition calling for debt cancellation for the 37 poorest countries by the year 2000. This action was endorsed as a priority by the Forum of Churches Together in England in July 1997. Both at county level and more locally other projects are being identified that would involve sacrificial giving by the churches and make possible a new start for those marginalised within British society.

---

2.2 **Faith in Leeds – One City Project**[3] unites suburban and inner city churches in a shared response to the injustices of society. It includes visits to projects concerned with poverty, homelessness, alcohol and drug dependency, unemployment and racism; a Walk of Awareness; and a day in the city with only 50p to spend, with reflection and prayer before and afterwards.

---

2.3 **Grassroots Programme**[4] is a partnership in Mission involving people from the Third World. Churches are invited to listen and learn from those of other cultures and particularly those who represent the poor and marginalised.

---

2.4 **Milton Keynes Ecumenical Peace and Justice Group**[5] has consciously decided to employ a development worker from India so that people here in Britain can appreciate his perspective on Justice, Peace and Integrity of Creation issues. This helps churches to explore mission, to become committed to working for justice, to share new ways of worshipping, to discover new ways of Bible study, to recognise the importance of creating churches which are open to all newcomers and to celebrate the gifts which belong to the people of God.

---

2.5 **The Change Group in Telford**[6] – associated with Telford Christian Council – is involved with industrialists, the university, the Green Party and others in alternative visioning of an economic system which is not dominated by global capitalism. It has campaigned for the teaching of ethics in schools, has registered its concern about the way that the interest rate is used to fine-tune the economy and is working on alterative pension provision concepts. It also supports small-scale local alternative ventures such as a Caribbean Food Co-operative.

---

2.6 Monitoring the effects of the Asylum & Immigration Act 1996 and mobilising support for refugee communities and asylum seekers is being undertaken by groups in **London** and **Oxfordshire**. For example, Anglicans, Catholics and Methodists are all involved in the work of the Karibu Day Centre based at the Vauxhall Mission, meeting emergency needs of those who lost all entitlement to benefits and housing as a result of the Act. Asylum Welcome and Detainee Support based in Oxford monitors the work of Campsfield House Kidlington, where many asylum seekers are held in detention while their cases are investigated.[7]

2.7 All the churches are committed to working for racial justice but it is easy for rural areas in particular to say "It is not our problem".

A 1994 report tackling the invisibility of racism in **Norfolk** discovered that there was an immigrant family in two-thirds of the villages in the county. The family might be black, Asian, Romany, from the Irish Republic or from mainland Europe.

Representatives of Churches Together groups can be active in Racial Equality Councils and in combatting xenophobia in all its forms.

A leaflet, *Race Relations and Racial Justice – Issues for Christians in **Devon***, suggests several possible courses of action for local churches, Christian groups or individuals.[8]

2.8 Churches Together groups can work with national campaign movements – holding 'Hearings' in association with **Church Action on Poverty**.[9]

2.9 Many towns have responded to the problem of homelessness. A number of housing assocations formed by councils of churches have made a very significant contribution to housing people with special needs.

In **Bath** a temporary night shelter was run in a church hall; then in the basement of the Baptist Church. Eventually a purpose-built night shelter was built in the redevelopment of the Baptist buildings, and run in a strongly developed way by Bath Churches Housing Association. It includes a drop-in centre some mornings, and over 20 beds are available every night. It is comparatively well furnished, and financed by the local Council, housing benefit and voluntary fund-raising, which has to produce £150,000 per year. A project is under way for a 'half-way house' – it is found that individual flats work less effectively.

In addition, Churches Together in Bath run an 'Open Christmas' at a local school. Guests are transported in; food is free; the Queen's Speech is shown on a large screen. Some of the volunteers are lonely themselves and meet their own needs by serving others. A local person said, "Churches Together in Bath took off after this event".

---

2.10 In **Wallasey**, the Social Responsibility Committee of Wallasey Council of Churches was alerted to the needs of the homeless and set up the first 'Ark'. Now it is a hostel for young adults aged 18-25; 64 churches are involved, with 200 volunteers from Wallasey and Birkenhead on a rota. Ark has 'Ten Commandments' which are firmly enforced. Drugs and alcohol have to be handed in on arrival, and are returned on leaving. Pensioners are the backbone of the volunteer force. There is no Council funding, as it is said that they would want strings attached. Ark runs during the winter months, but is working towards funding for a year-round operation. Its present location is in **Birkenhead**.

---

2.11 In **Newark** the local Council of Churches (now a Churches Together group) was instrumental in establishing an 'Emmaus' community. There are further such communities in **Cambridge, Coventry, Greenwich, Dover** and **Brighton** and more are planned. The first Emmaus was set up in France. The Abbé Pierre took some homeless people into his home; numbers grew, bigger premises were needed and a community of 'ragpickers' was formed, earning their living by recycling and selling many things which other people threw away. Homeless people thus cease to be dependent and are given a way of earning what they need, company instead of solitude and restored self-respect. The recycling work that they do is now recognised as something valuable for the environment.[10]

---

2.12 Churches Together in **Carlisle** runs an effective One World Forum/ Centre. This is an annexe at the buildings of the Church of Scotland in the city centre, entitled 'DOVES'. In February 1995 a coffee lounge was opened together with a fair trade shop. It employs two part-time staff and has recruited 80 volunteers from 12 churches to run the venture. Prices are kept low to ensure use by those on low income – sometimes free snacks are offered to destitute individuals. It is open from Monday to Friday, 10.00am to 2.00pm; 10% of the income goes to One World/Third World projects – £1,200 was distributed in the first ten months. In the summer of 1995 a One World Forum was formed by Churches Together in Carlisle, comprising representatives of congregations interested in social and international issues. It has given oversight to the coffee lounge, shared information on One World issues, organised events around One World topics, hunger lunches, Lenten meetings on health and wholeness, and co-ordinated Christian Aid Week. Since 1996, CTC has used part of the budget to appoint an honorary secretary (paid £1000 per annum) to service and develop the activities of the Forum. This appointment has been made and has proved very successful.

## 3.0 Some ecumenical responses to promote Peace

3.1 **Campaign Against the Arms Trade**[11] has particular relevance in those areas where arms manufacture is a significant part of the local economy or where 'arms fairs' are regularly held. Will local churches feel able to campaign under a Churches Together banner on such issues? Can they pray publicly for individuals whose consciences compel them to take direct action, e.g. damage to fighter planes about to be exported to Indonesia? The Religious Society of Friends,[12] noted and admired for espousing a positive peace stance, is a good source of information and contacts and the local Friends' Meeting can be a valued stimulus to other Christians in the area to tackle such issues.

3.2 In some places people meet together in one church after morning service to write letters about **prisoners of conscience** whose details have been publicised by Amnesty International.[13] The sending of Christmas cards to political prisoners and their families is a simple act of solidarity which is highly valued.

3.3 **Landmines Campaign**: Many groups were involved in CAFOD's[14] landmine campaign begun in 1995, a significant success is signalled by the announcement by the UK Government in May 1997 of an immediate ban on the manufacture, transfer, import and export of anti-personnel mines and of the destruction of British stockpiles by 2005. Pressure needs to be maintained to secure international funding for the systematic clearing of landmines.

3.4 **The Programme to Combat Violence**[15] was the brainchild of the Revd Stanley Mogoba, a Methodist Bishop in South Africa, who told member churches of the World Council of Churches': "the churches worldwide have helped us to do away with the evil of apartheid but the evil of growing violence in my country, and in yours, must be challenged and combatted too." Violence is an issue at a personal, community, national and international level. A pack available from Council of Churches for Britain & Ireland can form the basis of a workshop or series of workshops. Many local Christians are concerned to address issues such as bullying, vandalism and mugging and to understand what lies behind them.

---

3.5 **Hall Green** Council of Churches in Birmingham has since 1984 been hosting each July a group of children drawn from both Catholic and Protestant communities in **Northern Ireland**. The main object is enabling young people to mix in a neutral, stress-free atmosphere. This gives an opportunity for them to extend their horizons and to experience the love and care of strangers who are also Christian and to realise that it is possible to share together that which at home divides. The link is with an estate known as New Mossley, some seven miles north-west of Belfast. On the first holiday the Catholic children were bussed to Larne to catch the ferry while the Protestants came in a separate bus. On their return all the youngsters insisted on sharing buses. The holiday project has been the cement holding together the churches in Hall Green. It has also resulted in the formation of Churches Together in New Mossley.

---

## 4.0 Some ecumenical responses to ecological issues

4.1 **Yew Trees for the Millennium**[16] was launched by the Archbishop of York and David Bellamy in September 1996. **The Conservation Foundation** has identified the oldest yew trees in Britain including 500 which are at least 2000 years old. Cuttings from these ancient trees have been nurtured so that in each parish a tree can be planted to mark the 2000th anniversary of the birth of Jesus Christ. While often it will be appropriate to plant the young yew tree in the grounds of the parish church, it would be good if the decision were taken ecumenically - and it may be appropriate for other churches to plant them too.

4.2 **Agenda 21**: Many local authorities have set up local Agenda 21 groups pursuing matters raised at the Rio Earth Summit in 1992. Sustainability is the key word. In a number of areas the local Churches Together is a significant partner, e.g. **Hastings**. Churches which have sizeable grounds or a churchyard are challenged to develop them in an environmentally friendly way. The Arthur Rank Centre's 'Living Churchyard' programme highlighted what could be done.[17]

4.3 **Cheshire's Agenda 21 Inter-Faith Group**, which supports the work of the Sustainable Cheshire Forum has produced its own leaflet.[18] This includes a check list which is set out below –

❶ recycled/environmentally friendly paper is used for parish newsletters etc.

❷ Fair Trade goods, e.g. coffee, are purchased for all church activities.

❸ There are church collections of aluminium cans, paper etc. to support recycling (and gain funds).

❹ An energy saving campaign is in place, including low-energy lighting, heating controls etc. for all church buildings.

❺ Regular prayers are said for environmental concerns and a 'green' harvest festival held annually.

❻ Encouragement is given to placing church money on deposit with 'green'/ethical funds.

❼ Each church group has decided what it can do to help 'green' the locality, so contributing to Conservation Sunday in June and One World Week in October.

❽ Wild flowers and wild life are encouraged on church land and other open spaces. A tree is planted each year on behalf of the churches.

❾ People are encouraged to walk or cycle to church regularly and especially on Conservation Sunday.

❿ Local community organic food ventures are supported and organic communion bread and wine used.

> 4.3 **Environmental competitions:** In 1995 the Northumbria Police and the Northumbrian Water Company ran a competition for youth groups and schools entitled the 'Square Mile'. This was an environmental project and involved groups adopting a 'square mile' of their locality and looking after it from the point of view of collecting litter, getting permission to paint murals on derelict walls, or writing letters to interested parties. Two church groups, both representing Local Ecumenical Partnerships, reached the **Durham** county finals, **Woodhouse Close Bishop Auckland** being the eventual regional winners.

## 5.0    Churches Together or Pressure Group?

5.1 Often the Churches Together group will have a key role in initiating and sustaining a significant piece of work bearing on justice, peace or creation issues. It is not always easy to judge at what point a particular work should become autonomous or be passed over to another agency in a similar field. Perhaps the project should cease to exist because the need is no longer there or its pilot nature has served its turn.

5.2 Many local groups of Churches Together are committed to working in a variety of styles, sometimes hands-on and sometimes more tenuously, perhaps through one representative serving on a board of trustees.

5.3 The **verbs** used in the 1997 Churches Together in Central Oxford leaflet to describe its own role illustrates well this variety of ways of working: *"Churches Together in Central Oxford welcomes all visitors and newcomers to worship in any of its member churches. This leaflet gives details of the main Sunday services and a contact from whom further information may be obtained. There are opportunities for joint prayer during the group's quarterly meetings and in Christian Unity Week and in some churches during Holy Week. Churches Together in Central Oxford co-operates with the Oxfordshire Ecumenical Council, participates in the Women's World Day of Prayer, and has recently appointed a City Chaplain (tel...) to minister to those working in the city centre. CTC also runs The Gatehouse (tel.), a drop-in centre for homeless people, and supports Oxford Black and White Christian Partnership through Asylum Welcome and Detainee Support (AWADS), currently at St. Columba's (tel ...)."*

--------------------------------------------------------------------------------

**FOOTNOTES**:

1. The Five Marks of Mission – see Chapter 2, 7.1.

2. Jubilee 2000: information from Christian Aid, CAFOD, Tear Fund etc (addresses below).

3. Faith in Leeds: One City Project, 53 Cardigan Lane, Leeds, LS4 2LE.

4. Grassroots Programme: Chapel Street Centre, 15/17 Chapel Street, Luton, LU1 2SE.

5. Milton Keynes Peace and Justice Centre, 300 Saxon Gate West, Central Milton Keynes, MK9 2ES.

6. The Change Group in Telford, Mr. F. Selkirk, 42 Church Street, Broseley, Shropshire, TF12 5BX.

7. Asylum Welcome and Detainee Support, St. Columba's United Reformed Church, Alfred Street, Oxford.

8. *Race Relations & Racial Justice: Issues for Christians in Devon*, Social Responsibility Committee, Board for Christian Care, 96 Old Tiverton Road, Exeter, EX4 6LD.

9. Church Action on Poverty, Central Buildings, Oldham Street, Manchester M1 1JT.

10. Emmaus Communities: Emmaus UK, 4 Salisbury Villages, Station Road, Cambridge, CB1 2JF.

11. Campaign Against the Arms Trade, 11 Goodwins Street, London N4 3HQ.

12. Quaker Peace and Service, Friends House, Euston Road, London NW1 2BJ.

13. Amnesty International, British Section, 99-119 Rosebery Avenue, London EC1R 4RE.

14. CAFOD, (Catholic Fund for Overseas Development), Romero Close, Stockwell Road, London SW9 9TY.

15. Programme to Combat Violence, c/o Norman Kember, Churches Peace Forum Working Group, 35-41 Lower Marsh, London SE1 7RL. or Helen Drewery, QSRE, Friends House, Euston Road, London NW1 2BJ.

16. Yew Trees for the Millennium, The Conservation Foundation, 1 Kensington Gore, London SW7 2AR.

17. Living Churchyards, Arthur Rank Centre, Stoneleigh Park, Warwickshire, CV8 2LZ.

18. Cheshire Agenda 21, Revd Dr Brian Powley, 5 Sandside Road, Alsager, ST7 2XJ.

## 14. CHURCHES DEVELOPING INTERNATIONAL LINKS TOGETHER

### 1.0 Universal Reconciliation – A Local Task

1.1 Christians are called to continue the reconciling work of Christ, so that the household of God may be reunited. A sign, instrument and foretaste of this kingdom-yet-to-be-realised is the Church – one, holy, catholic and apostolic. International linking between Christians is a natural way of expressing the catholicity/universality of the Church. The search for the unity of the Church locally – transcending denominational barriers – and the development of a sense of the universal Church – transcending national distinctions – may go hand in hand. Both may involve the out-lawing of prejudice and the healing of memories; both may involve the joy of reconciliation and the richness of diversity.

1.2 International responsibility for one another – bearing one another's burdens – is the fulfilment of the law of Christ, the law of loving one's neighbour. Locally, that responsibility is to be shared by Christians and churches working together.

1.3 It is remarkable how easy it is to overlook the presence and contribution of people from other parts of the world living and working either short- or long-term in one's own community. Hospitality to international students is an obvious way in which local Christians can cross cultural divides and create ties of Christian friendship.[1] Where there is a local congregation drawn primarily from a minority ethnic group, e.g. Greek Orthodox, culture and faith will be closely bound together. A social evening or weekend featuring its distinctive contribution should be considered.

1.4 Many denominations encourage local churches to invite missionaries who are home on furlough and there are programmes for exchange of clergy during the summer. Can opportunities be found for them to feature on the ecumenical scene? The Methodist Church and the United Reformed Church invite ministers from other parts of the world to serve in local ministry in Britain. Such ministers are eager to work ecumenically and will have a special perspective to offer. Some of them come from united or uniting churches.

### 2.0 Relating ecumenically

2.1 In many respects relationships between churches in England in the last years of the twentieth century are better than the equivalent relationships in most other countries. Care needs to be taken that it is an ecumenical spirit and experience which is exported, not a denominational one. Some denominations are so internationally organised that they may not feel an immediate need for further links. Some denominations may give to agreements between themselves and churches abroad a greater significance than do those churches abroad. Some churches may be tempted to ignore in international relations the denominational disciplines which pertain at home. International links may be easier, less threatening and more glamorous than ecumenical relations at home.

## 3.0 Aid/development relief

3.1 Christian Aid and CAFOD (Catholic Fund for Overseas Development) are increasingly working together nationally, and local co-operation can be developed. Tear Fund links specifically with evangelical churches, and may provide a point of contact with churches not always in the vanguard of local ecumenical relations. Joint efforts should be considered. In many places the Roman Catholics play a full part in Christian Aid Week house-to-house collections in May. In an increasing number of places other churches are sharing in the CAFOD Family Fast Days in March and October.

3.2 Many places have been active in providing relief to the struggling countries of Eastern Europe, particularly Bosnia and Romania. Such common concern has drawn local churches closer together here, with regular collections of clothing, toiletries and basic stationery items being arranged and driven across Europe by lorry, often by members of local churches themselves.

## 4.0 Taizé and the Kirchentag

4.1 In their different ways, Taizé in France and the Kirchentag in Germany provide inspiration and encouragement to those seeking an ecumenical vision. Both can usefully be a focus of pilgrimage and a source of enrichment to local church groupings, and may be especially appealing to younger people. There is a Taizé Gathering in a major European city each year just after Christmas.

4.2 The Kirchentag began as a assembly of lay Protestant Christians seeking a new way forward after the Second World War. It is now held in a major German city every two years, the largest regular Christian gathering in the world. An estimated 107,000 people gathered in Leipzig in June 1997. Appropriately the Bishop of Birmingham, Leipzig's twin city, preached at an opening service. The Kirchentag is essentially open to all who want to attend, those under 25 are in the majority but everyone is welcome. It has been called it "a mixture of a Bible convention, Taize, Greenbelt, an Open University Summer School, a Synod, two Edinburgh Festivals (and three Fringes), an Eisteddfod, a brass band festival, a Swanwick conference, an Ideal Home Exhibition and a Cup Final, all rolled into one and going on at the same time!" In alternate years there is a (Catholic) Katholikentag. It is hoped that by 2005 they may be fully integrated.

## 5.0 Twinnings and exchanges

5.1 Many congregation-to-congregation twinnings come about informally, through the enthusiasm of a few individuals – perhaps the ministers. These may be fragile links, endangered when individuals move elsewhere.

5.2 Some Dioceses, Districts and Provinces have links with Dioceses or Districts abroad, though not strictly their equivalents. It is important to be aware of these links, and to explore whether they could be extended to become ecumenical. If a large unit (e.g. Diocese) has a link, can the smaller units of individual congregations twin with congregations abroad? Churches Together in **Derbyshire** has developed a strong relationship with the Church of North India, with groups of young people exchanging visits.

5.3 Many cities, towns and villages have civic twinnings. Can the churches link as well, council of churches/Churches Together grouping to their equivalents abroad, or congregations to congregations? By so doing, a new depth may be brought to the civic twinning, and the home churches may even meet people in their locality whom they would not otherwise have known.

> **Churches Together in High Barnet**, for example, is twinned with Siegand Rhein Church District in Germany, the link covering church life, mission, ecumenical and economic concerns.
>
> Both partners have contributed to a piece of World Council of Churches research exploring what fosters a missionary congregation.

5.4 'Twinnings' may extend to further partners – the churches of the former West Germany have 'twins' in the eastern part, so three-way relationships (and even more) may be achieved.

> 5.5 **Churches Together in Leeds** has a strong developing relationship with Dortmund, Germany, which led to an international ecumenical service commemorating VE Day in Leeds in May 1995. Christians from Leeds attended the Graz 2nd European Ecumenical Assembly with their Dortmund friends.

> 5.6 **Churches Together in the Borough of Croydon** has, since 1989, developed a strong network of links; beginning with a visit to Arnhem, Holland, in 1989 – leading to a conference in Budapest, Hungary, in 1992; a visit to Lodz, Poland, in 1994. In 1995 CTBC produced a policy statement expressing commitment to continuing links with many parts of Europe, including Holland, Germany, Hungary, Poland and Romania.

> 5.7 The **Coventry – Dresden** link is well known, and has moved from an Anglican link to an ecumenical one; in 1990, fifty years after the bombing of Coventry and forty-five years after the bombing of Dresden, an ecumenical group from Coventry City Centre Covenanting Churches visited their counterparts in Dresden.

> 5.8 The **Melksham/Marienhafe Twinning Association** has been exchanging visits for over twenty years and since 1989 the Melksham Family of Churches has been formally a part of the association as has the Lutheran district of Brookmerland. A Marienhafe ordinand who had been part of a youth exchange did a two-month youth worker placement in Melksham as part of his pre-college training. Subsequently the County Ecumenical Officer attended his ordination in Germany. He is now working as area youth officer and Deacon in Norden which happens to be twinned with Bradford on Avon, another Wiltshire town, so it is hoped that the contacts will grow.

5.9 Within the twinnings, there may be opportunities for exchange of expertise, of specialist interest groups, of theological study. The value of joint worship cannot be over-emphasised, and a resource of multi-lingual material is being built up. Most important is the extension of participation. This is not a tour for the elite, but a rich experience of unity in diversity.

"It is always easier to love at a distance than to love the person near to hand, but twinnings and exchanges should also help us to get to know our separated brothers and sisters on our own doorsteps".[2] The thrill of international *koinonia* may enliven faith, life and witness in the Churches Together locally.

-------------------------------------------------------------------------------------------------

## FOOTNOTES:

1. The Churches Commission on Overseas Students, 1 Stockwell Green, London, SW9 9HP, has a leaflet *"Learning to Share"* giving basic information about international students in Britain and what local churches and individuals can do to welcome them.

2. *Twinnings and Exchanges* – Guidelines proposed by Anglican-Roman Catholic Committees of France and England, 1990; page 12. Church House Bookshop, Great Smith Street, London SW1 3NZ.

**Other Resources:**

*European Church Partnership* – Robin Blout, 1994, CAFE (Christianity and the Future of Europe) Westcott House, Cambridge CB5 8BP.

*In Spirit and In Truth,* 2 volumes: Hymns and Responses; Prayers to the Holy Spirit. WCC 1991.

*Worshipping Ecumenically* – ed. Per Harling, WCC. (Orders of Service from Global Meetings with Suggestions for Local Use).

*Celebrating Community,* WCC 1993.

## 15. CHURCHES USING RESOURCES TOGETHER

### 1.0 Common spiritual resources

1.1 In the power of the Holy Spirit, local churches draw on the same fundamental spiritual resources – the gospel, the Holy Scriptures, prayer and sacraments. Increasingly they may draw on each other's insights into spirituality, nurture, biblical scholarship and training methods. They also recognise that they are sharers in God's common mission and need to reach out in evangelism and service to their locality and in challenging injustice. This sharing is fundamental to the growth of Christian unity.

1.2 As Christians we recognise that God-given resources are to be used to the full, in responsible stewardship. If, under God, we are committed to each other's good, we should increasingly be putting our resources of people, money, plant and equipment at the disposal of partner churches, as far as is legally and practically possible.

### 2.0 People/Personnel

2.1 Sharing ministry releases resources. It can release the precious commodity of time, release financial restrictions, release pressure on accommodation and release people. This can enable other issues/challenges to be tackled.

2.2 There are many possibilities of sharing 'people resources'. Where relations of real trust have developed Anglicans look to Methodists and vice-versa to provide cover for each other when either the minister or priest is away. In Local Ecumenical Partnerships a measure of interchangeability of clergy is possible. Encouragement should be given to developing the sense of sharing both clergy and lay resources in Churches Together groupings.[1]

In its response to *Called To Be One* Churches Together in **Lancashire** made the following telling comment:– "If local clergy were to be seen much more as serving and belonging to all the churches, not only of their own denomination, it would greatly help progress towards unity".

2.3 Leaders for Quiet Days, Retreats, Weeks of Guided Prayer can be drawn from across the denominations. Information from the National Retreat Association.[2]

2.4 When a Methodist/URC church was holding a stewardship campaign, which included a special meal to which every member was invited, their Baptist neighbours offered to prepare and serve the meal so that the objective could be achieved.

2.5 There could be more interchange of readers, lay and local preachers. We should keep each other informed and pray for the concerns of neighbouring churches in public worship. Someone in each church could be chosen as a contact for subjects for intercession. The need to pray systematically in Sunday worship for churches in the locality and their leaders was deemed a priority by the Churches Together in England Forum, July 1997.[3]

## 3.0 Buildings

3.1 Church buildings are frequently under-used. A Sharing Agreement under the Sharing of Church Buildings Act, 1969, enables one building to be used as if it were simultaneously a church of another denomination and makes provision for proper apportionment of running costs etc.[4] Even where a formal Agreement may not be appropriate, there are often ways in which intelligent use of buildings can further the churches' mission.

3.2 There are successful examples of sharing where churches in a locality have complementary buildings.

> In **Loddon**, Norfolk, the ancient and beautiful parish church is used for Sunday worship in summer, and the Methodist chapel in winter as it is much cosier and cheaper to heat. The Roman Catholic congregation also meets throughout the year in the Methodist building, but at a separate time.

3.3 The opportunities to make available church buildings to other Christian groups are many, whether for social or training events or for services. Requests may be made, particularly by black-majority churches, for the use of a Baptist church with its baptistry for the baptism of believers by total immersion. New or black majority churches, regularly meeting in secular buildings, may ask to hold a wedding in a church building.

It is important to note that there are two distinct systems for registering weddings in England, one covering Church of England buildings and clergy and the other covering churches of other denominations. This means that Church of England churches are legally unable to host weddings conducted by non-Anglican clergy.[5] The Free Churches do not necessarily have the same constraints. Understanding between the local clergy as to their policy and practice would enable a helpful response to be given by any church receiving such requests.

3.4 'Host church' and 'guest church' are terms now in current usage due to the increase of requests by other worshipping groups to hold regular services on church premises. Useful and important guidelines are given in the leaflet *Sharing and Sale of Church Buildings.*[6] Sharing buildings can lead to as many problems as it solves. Clarity, openness, trust and consideration are vital from all concerned.

3.5 When faced with a proposed sale of a church building it is worth considering possibilities of joint use.

> In **Crosby**, when a church with a most strategic site was on the point of closure, the local covenanted churches planned a conversion into a café and counselling centre, staffed jointly from all the churches. One denomination's building and the vision and personnel of sister churches enabled a very valuable piece of Christian service to be launched.

3.6 When the United Reformed Church united with the Methodists to form Christchurch, **Newmarket** in 1994, the vacated URC building was developed into a community resource – *the Stable* – in the heart of Newmarket High Street. After wide consultation over 12 months with voluntary and statutory groups it was decided to create a safe 'centre for care' free from alcohol and drugs and open to all individuals and groups. Over £60,000 came from Methodist and URC sources and from other local churches as well as from the Forest Heath District Council. A part-time paid manager was appointed and over 40 volunteers recruited and trained. There is an under-20s evening on Fridays and some of the youngsters also drop in on Saturday mornings. The hall is regularly used for professional Christian drama productions, seminars, regional church gatherings, and by twelve caring agencies.

## 4.0 Finance, Administration and Communication

4.1 Those who have responsibility for local church money and property are key people. The saying that "people's pockets are often the hardest thing to convert" can sadly be true of ecumenism also. Ecumenism and Economics are both about caring for God's house (*oikos*). A wider concept of the household of faith can make good financial sense. Unless those having responsibility for the material aspects of church life are prepared to ask the ecumenical question, little progress will be made.

4.2 There is a tendency for each congregation to want to be independent in these matters, but availability of photocopiers, printers and people to produce the newsletter/magazine can be problematical, particularly for smaller churches and in villages. A well produced joint churches' magazine could be an invaluable witness for the group involved and have the credibility to be placed in libraries, doctors' and dentists' surgeries, and other local centres.

4.3 The Church Urban Fund (Church of England) and Resourcing Mission which continues to promote Mission Alongside the Poor (the Methodist equivalent) are valuable sources of advice and funding, especially when it is evident that there is a shared will to tackle deprivation. Opportunities for Volunteering, an agency of Churches Together in England, makes grants for church-based projects working in their local community. Applications to fund ecumenical initiatives are warmly invited.[7]

4.4 In any area, but especially in old established market towns, there will be local charities which can be approached for funding for imaginative work. The vicar will often be a trustee ex officio!

4.5 It is also worth approaching local firms whether large or small to sponsor ecumenically planned events or undertakings.

A major supermarket chain is on record as donating five hundred loaves with which to carry out a delicate cleaning operation on a church in **Andover** badly damaged by fire!

4.6 Regional tourist boards will gladly advise on publicity for church open days, pilgrimage trails etc. and may well undertake the cost of publishing leaflets.

Achieving this requires the kind of joint decision-making described in Chapter 5.

## 5.0 Community Outreach

5.1 It is important to ensure that the essential initial audit of resources, people, plant and finances in relation to the community being served is carried out.[8]

5.2 The work of trusts and agencies operating in a particular field should be drawn on and not replicated. However, it is useful to investigate an initiative somewhere else which may have much to teach. It is always a good idea to learn from others' success and even better to learn from their mistakes. This is well illustrated in the story of **Horsham** Christian Centre which, as it illuminates virtually every chapter in this handbook, is recounted in Appendix I.

5.3 Tensions often arise between 'non-denominational' initiatives, supported by evangelical individuals and congregations, and programmes formally promoted by Churches Together groupings. In a large urban area there may be room for a variety of approaches but it is not as easy in a smaller place, where it is hard to disguise polarised attitudes. In at least one large city there is mutual representation on the 'umbrella' council of churches' executive and the council of the city-wide grouping of evangelical churches. At least each can then know what the other is doing and planning. Churches Together groupings may be placed in a difficult situation if they are asked to endorse or sponsor an initiative that is already in place. There are no easy answers to this, each decision has to be taken on its merits.

## 6.0 Music and Drama

6.1 Music is rightly seen as of great significance in enabling people to engage more wholeheartedly in worship  since the body and the emotions as well as the mind are involved. Many churches do not have a regular choir and would value the opportunity of more varied and competent musical input to worship from time to time.

---

The **Wath-upon-Dearne** Council of Churches recruits a choir which meets regularly and prepares cantatas which it then offers to perform to mark special occasions in the life of any of the local churches.

---

6.2 *Called to Be Fun* was the title of the Saturday evening revue at the Churches Together in England Forum in July 1997 which provided much pungent though light-hearted comment on ecumenical attitudes and misconceptions. Sketches featured in *All Year Round* [9] have been found a useful resource not only for joint worship but also for local inter-church social occasions.

## 7.0 Greater Integration

7.1 In order to secure the maximum integration of resources it is worth contemplating becoming a Local Ecumenical Partnership (LEP) of the Covenanted Congregations in Partnership variety.[10] This could allow ministry to be exercised and capital money to be ported across denominational boundaries.

However, the fact that the ministers get on well and share an impatience with denominational structures is not justification for LEP status. The desire to build securely on an already firm foundation must be shared by a sizeable proportion of each congregation, too. Better a really good local Churches Together grouping than an ineffective and aimless Covenanted Congregations in Partnership LEP!

----------------------------------------------------------------------------------------------

### FOOTNOTES:

1. See 7 below.

2. National Retreat Association, Central Hall, 256 Bermondsey Street, London SE1 3UJ.

3. See Chapter 8, 9.1.

4. *Under the Same Roof: Guidelines to the Sharing of Church Buildings Act, 1969* CCBI, 1994.

5. The existence of a Sharing Agreement is a prerequisite for enabling non-Anglican weddings to be held in a Church of England church. See Note 3 above.

6. Sale and Sharing of Church Buildings, CTE 1993.

7. Opportunities for Volunteering, Inter-Church House, 35-41 Lower Marsh, London SE1 7RL.

8. See Chapters 10, 11 and 12.

9. *All Year Round,* CCBI Publications.

10. For further information about Local Ecumenical Partnerships see *Travelling Together,* Welch & Winfield, CTE (Publications) 1995 and/or contact CTE Field Officers or County Ecumenical Officers.

## I  A NEW CHRISTIAN CENTRE FOR HORSHAM

### *A Case Study in patient ecumenical co-operation*

In March 1995 a new base for Christian outreach was opened by the Horsham Churches, with a coffee shop and a book shop upstairs meeting needs within and beyond the churches.

### Conception of the project

The project was conceived at the time of ecumenical Lenten house groups organised in 1990 by what was then the Horsham Council of Churches. In a plenary session after Easter most speakers came with a suggestion that the Council should seriously consider setting up some kind of 'drop-in' centre in town. Alongside this was a note of sadness that the Christian book shop which had proved useful over the years had closed at Easter because the people running it felt the call to use their gifts in different ways. So, the question also came, "Could a book shop be a part of this venture?"

### Churches working together

Part of the background to this initiative was the increasing level of co-operation among the churches of Horsham with a wide membership of the Council of Churches and an even wider representation of different churches at the Ministers' Fraternal. About 20 churches are members of the Council and the Fraternal often gathers 25 members of the local clergy, some of whose churches may not feel entirely at ease with or ready to join the Council are happy to meet.

For the rest of 1990 the proposal was held in the minds and prayers of individuals and churches. In January 1991 one of the ministers, who had previously worked in Beaconsfield, led a small group of people to see the progress of a project which he had assisted in founding. Knowledge gained through that expedition formed the basis of much that followed.

In the May a meeting took place at which this knowledge was shared with about 80 members of the different churches. There was total support from them urging the group to take the matter further. The September meeting of the Council of Churches adopted a statement of the aims of the proposed centre and set up an ad hoc group.

### A time of Testing and a rekindled Vision into 1992

This became a time of testing. Some of the initial enthusiasm had worn off, the search for the ideal premises drew a blank and the realistic estimates of costs started to look prohibitive. It was with the setting up of a prayer group and then the introduction on the scene of various other people with visions of their own that turned the near despondency back into hope. Quite independently two people approached their ministers to share the vision of a call they believed they were receiving from God to do something in Horsham which sounded remarkably similar to what was being planned. This set the 'Feasibility Group' back to serious consideration of the venture. The individuals who had thought God was calling them to set up a shop as a family business were persuaded by the research already done that the costs were prohibitive and that it would be far better to bring in as many volunteers as possible from all the churches. This would be harder to achieve if people felt there were merely cheap labour supporting a family or individual. However, instead of leaving the group to get on with it the individuals were very keen to be involved and joined the group.

## Funding

It was soon recognised that, the shop would involve financial risk. From the outset it had been hoped that all the churches of Horsham would share the responsibilities for the project according to their respective sizes and that it would truly be a Churches Together project. However several churches felt unable to enter into the project quite so deeply. Two or three also felt they had so much on their own agendas that they would be unable to do the project justice. Reluctantly it was agreed that a core group of churches would have to own the project while Churches Together would still be involved with its Chairman as Chairman of the Board.

For the initial fund-raising it was originally hoped that about £40,000 would be sufficient to begin. Churches were given target figures based on their respective memberships for their contributions. These ranged from £750 to £14,000. It was made clear to all that participation did not depend on meeting these targets, they were for guidance, but it was also made clear that the money was needed. In the event all the participating churches met or bettered their targets and in addition raised money from special events and memorials.

With these funds promised, the business was officially constituted and a group of Trustees/Directors elected. The trustees first met in May 1993. Applications were made for registration as a business and as a charity. Then the search began in earnest for suitable premises. This was perhaps the most trying time. Every property would involve compromises and the best would involve even higher costs than anticipated. Eventually the sum required turned out to be more than double the first estimate. Already individuals had given interest-free loans and a few sizeable gifts. It was agreed not to ask the churches as such to increase their investments but to go for further loans and gifts. The response turned out to be almost exactly equal to the need.

## Premises

Much of the first year of the board of directors was taken up with finding premises. We were looking for something central and it was going to be expensive. We also found it was going to take money and a lot of groundwork. With several false starts having been made, interested members of churches had been teased with different possibilities for opening dates and were given further reason to doubt that it would ever start.

Negotiations began in mid 1993 for the property at 3-5 South Street. This building was about 300 years old and had seen use as a pub, a tea shop, a book shop and an estate agents. This one seemed right from the start. The pre-Christmas trade in 1993 was anticipated as setting the launch date, until negotiations dragged into mid 1994 and the architect's report prescribed three months' work on the structure. Despite the higher costs there was a resolve to go ahead. In mid 1994 when it was clear we would again be too late for the Christmas rush it was decided to look for a temporary start with half the proposed trade in another shop we were offered for a short term on a minimal rental.

The book shop in East Street gave the chance to establish working practices, to build up a clientele for the books, and to introduce the man who was to run the full project later on. By the time we moved into the South Street premises the book shop was almost running itself, leaving the manager to concentrate on the coffee shop side of the business.

## Volunteers

From the first meeting in 1992 people had been asked to enlist as volunteers for work in the shop. By now that list was rather out of date. Also, while the members of the committee and those 'in the know' were aware of the progress, many of those who had originally offered were despairing of it ever taking off.

Various newsletters had been circulated but often these had the effect of causing more concern when they asked again for the same people to fill in yet another form to offer their services. When the book shop opened in phase one enough volunteers were found, but it was clear that many more were going to be needed when the coffee shop opened. From the outset one of the goals of the project was already being fulfilled: members of different Christian denominations discovered each other through working together. By August 1997 there were 90 volunteers.

## Barriers come down

An Anglican volunteer was asked for a recommendation for a gift for a customer's Roman Catholic friend. *"What about this book on Jesus?"* she proffered. *"Oh, but Catholics don't believe in Jesus do they?"* Another misconception was quietly overcome. A visitor to the coffee shop sat alone and began a conversation with a man on the next table. After expressing strong anti-church sentiments she said, *"But I do like coming here because this place has such a good atmosphere"* !

## Listening

We feel it is very important that the shop becomes known as a place where people can give time to others particularly if they have a need to be heard. The clergy of the participating churches have met regularly to determine how this should be done. We were fortunate in bringing in Acorn Christian Healing Trust to tailor a course on listening for us. All volunteers attend the basic listening course. A separate room on the top floor has been made available where people who need to talk on a confidential basis can be seen by appointment by one of the six or eight people with counselling experience. This room is also used for the regular prayer meeting every Friday, which is a vital part of the Centre's life.

## More recent progress

Early in 1996 a half-time catering manager was appointed. BBC Songs of Praise featured the Centre in September 1996 and this brought a huge response. More customers appeared – sales went up by 20% that month and have been maintained. More volunteers were forthcoming. The Centre broke even on week-by-week trading in 1996, a year ahead of target and in 1997 should begin to pay off some of its £50,000 outstanding loans.

The Centre has clearly become a focus for Churches Together in Horsham but also for the community as a whole.

*John Crocker & Stuart Bell*

# APPENDICES

## II(a) QUESTIONS TO ASK WHEN FORMING A GROUPING OF CHURCHES TOGETHER IN A NEIGHBOURHOOD OR SMALL TOWN

*These questions relate to "Draft Constitutional Guidelines for a Grouping of Churches Together in a Neighbourhood or Small Town" adopted by the Co-ordinating Group for Local Unity (GLU) in February 1996 (Appendix II(b)) The questions and the guidelines are offered to local groupings of churches setting up a Churches Together in X or changing from a Council of Churches mode.*

### 1. BASIS

Do we adopt the Churches Together in England Basis (see chapter 3.2.2)?

### 2. AIMS

Do all prospective members share the ecumenical vision spelt out in the Aims? Do we want to change the emphasis somewhat?

### 3. AREA

Have we got the **area** right? Does it follow natural boundaries? Does it split Catholic parishes? Should it include neighbouring villages?

### 4. RELATIONSHIPS

Have we liaised with our County Ecumenical Officer? Are we going to send agendas and minutes to the County Ecumenical Officer? Are we on the mailing list for ecumenical newsletters and CTE's *Pilgrim Post*?

### 5. MEMBERSHIP

Have we approached all the churches in the locality? In category (a)? In category (b)? In category (c)? (See Appendix 2b, para 5)
It is not a good witness if some churches take a step to deeper commitment and others are marginalised. If some local churches are hesitant, or dismissive, try to find out why. What is this telling us? Are they at least supportive of us in what we are doing? How can we develop relationships with them? Are there Christian organisations or projects in the locality which are not churches? As long as **most** of the members are churches, to include such groups will be an enrichment to the life of the Churches Together.

### 6. OFFICERS

These guidelines are self explanatory.

### 7. FORUM

What size of Forum are we looking for? Is there to be an Enabling Group/ Executive as well, in which case the forum could be larger?

## 8. ENABLING GROUP/EXECUTIVE

Should the churches be asked to appoint one representative each or should the Forum elect out of the total representation? How big should it be – a tight group may make for efficiency, a large one be more representative?

## 9. FINANCE

What level of funding do we need? What expectations are there? Will churches be challenged to provide extra funding for specific events or projects?
Have we an auditor who is external to the local churches?

## 10. CONSTITUTION

Has the draft been approved by all the prospective Member Churches?

## 11. REVIEW

Have we lodged a copy of the adopted Constitution with the County Ecumenical Officer? Does each church have a copy of the Constitution in its own Records?

## II(b) DRAFT CONSTITUTIONAL GUIDELINES FOR A GROUPING OF CHURCHES TOGETHER IN A NEIGHBOURHOOD OR SMALL TOWN

adopted by the Churches Co-ordinating Group for Local Unity of Churches Together in England in February 1996

*This document is to be regarded as advisory only and not definitive.*

*Comments are welcomed. You are advised to consult your County Ecumenical Officer before adopting a Churches Together in .......... Constitution and to send him/her a copy of the final document. Please also send a copy of the document to the appropriate Field Officer of Churches Together in England.*

### 1. BASIS

CHURCHES TOGETHER IN .......... unites in pilgrimage those Churches in .......... which, acknowledging God's revelation in Christ, confess the Lord Jesus Christ as God and Saviour according to the Scriptures, and, in obedience to God's will and in the power of the Holy Spirit commit themselves

– to seek a deepening of their communion with Christ and with one another in the Church, which is His body; and

– to fulfil their mission to proclaim the Gospel by common witness and service in the world

to the glory of the one God, Father, Son and Holy Spirit.

### 2. AIMS

The aims of Churches Together in .......... shall be –

(a) to enable the churches, as pilgrims together, to explore the Christian faith together, to develop mutual relationships, to seek a common mind, and to make decisions together;

(b) to encourage churches to worship, pray and reflect together on the nature and purpose of the church in the light of its mission – each church sharing with others the treasures of its tradition;

(c) to enable the churches to live and share the Gospel, to evangelise together and to take further steps towards fuller unity;

(d) to enable the churches to respond to the needs of society and to witness to the Gospel together.

### 3. AREA

Churches Together in .......... aims to serve either the neighbourhood of .......... or an area coterminous with .......... and .......... (specified parishes) or an area bounded by the ..... and the ..... (see attached map).

# 4. RELATIONSHIPS

Churches Together in .......... is in association with ...... County Ecumenical Council/Sponsoring Body/Churches Together in ..... County. (See Note 1)

# 5. MEMBERSHIP

Membership of Churches Together in .......... shall be open to –

(a) any local church in the area which is affiliated to a church or association of churches which a full member of Churches Together in England (see Note 2) **and**

(b) any other local church in the area which affirms the Basis and commits itself to promote the aims of Churches Together in .......... **and**

(c) any local church which on principle has no credal statements in its tradition and therefore cannot formally subscribe to the statement of faith in the Basis, provided that it satisfies 75% in number of those full member churches which subscribe to the Basis, that it manifests faith in Christ as witnessed to in the Scriptures and it is committed to the aims and purposes of Churches Together in .......... and that it will work in the spirit of the Basis. (See Note 3)

# 6. OFFICERS

The officers of Churches Together in .......... shall be a Moderator and a Deputy Moderator (one of whom shall normally be a minister and the other a lay person), an Honorary Treasurer and an Honorary Secretary (plus a Minute Secretary, if desired) to be elected at the Annual Meeting of the Forum. Officers shall serve for an initial period of (3) years and may be re-elected if willing to serve for one further period not exceeding (3) years.

# 7. FORUM

(a) The Forum shall consist of the clergy and ministers and up to ... others appointed from each participating church.

(b) The Forum may co-opt others; such co-options not exceeding 25% of the total number of representatives appointed by the participating churches.

(c) The Forum shall meet not less than ..... times annually. The ..... (month or season) meeting shall be the Annual Meeting at which the audited accounts shall be presented, officers elected, annual reports submitted and policy and initiatives for the year decided. Other meetings of the Forum shall be held as deemed desirable by the officers or at the written request of any (x number, e.g. three) of the participating church). At least two weeks notice in writing of any meeting of the Forum shall be given. (See Note 4) The attendance by at least one representative of at least half of the Member Churches shall constitute a quorum.

# 8. ENABLING GROUP/EXECUTIVE

(a) When there are more than six churches in membership of the Forum, the churches may appoint an Enabling Group/ Executive whose functions shall be to enable the member churches to make decisions in common and to serve as a reference point for the Forum.

(b) Where there is no Enabling Group/Executive the officers of the Forum shall fulfil this function.

(c) The Enabling Group/Executive shall comprise the officers of the Forum, up to four lay people, and up to four clergy or ministers appointed by the member churches with regard to an appropriate representation of the various Christian traditions and denominations in membership. Attendance by at least half of those eligible to be present shall constitute a quorum.

## 9. FINANCE

Each participating church/member body shall pay such annual sum to Churches Together in .......... as shall be agreed at the Annual Meeting of the Forum. The financial year shall be from .... (specify month) to .... (specify month). Cheques shall require the signature of any two of the four officers. An honorary auditor shall be appointed at the Annual Meeting.

## 10. CONSTITUTION

The constitution and any subsequent amendment to it requires the approval of 75% of the member churches, acting through their normal decision-making bodies. (See Note 5)

## 11. REVIEW

It is intended that Churches Together reflect the developing life of the Christian Churches as they continue their pilgrimage together. From time to time (every ... years) a Review Group shall be appointed by the member churches in consultation with the County Ecumenical Officer/County Sponsoring Body/Churches Together in ......... County to report on the progress of the pilgrimage and to make proposals for desirable changes.

## NOTES

1.Check with the CTE Field Officer whether there is an ecumenical body operating for your County or City region. If there is not, the following may be substituted as Article 4 of the Constitution:–

Churches Together in ....... and District is in association with Churches Together in England.

2. As at January 1998 the full members of Churches Together in England were –

      Baptist Union of Great Britain

      Cherubim and Seraphim Council of Churches

      Church of England

      Church of Scotland

      Congregational Federation

      Council of African & Afro-Caribbean Churches

      Council of Oriental Orthodox Christian Churches

      The Free Churches' Council

Greek Orthodox Church

Independent Methodist Churches

International Ministerial Council of Great Britain

Joint Council for Anglo-Caribbean Churches

Lutheran Council of Great Britain

Methodist Church

Moravian Church

New Testament Assembly

Religious Society of Friends

Roman Catholic Church

Russian Orthodox Church

Salvation Army

United Reformed Church

Wesleyan Holiness Church

Churches Together in England is open to receive applications for membership from other churches. Some local churches, which will on principle be unwilling to become a member of a national body because of their understanding of the church as local, may be willing to become members of local Churches Together.

3. Upon its inauguration Churches Together in England welcomed the Religious Society of Friends under clause 5(c) above.

4. It may prove helpful once or twice a year for the decision-making bodies of the member churches (e.g. the Parochial Church Council, the United Reformed Church Meeting) all to meet immediately prior to or immediately following the Forum on the same day. This would enable particular business of the Forum to be more closely related to the decisions of the member churches.

5. It cannot be over-emphasised that a major principle of the new ecumenical process is that it is the churches' own decision-making bodies, rather than simply a representative council acting on behalf of the churches, which need to make major ecumenical decisions about policy and priorities.

# APPENDICES

## III(a) QUESTIONS TO ASK WHEN FORMING AN UMBRELLA GROUPING OF CHURCHES TOGETHER FOR A SIZEABLE TOWN

*These questions relate to "Draft Constitutional Guidelines for an Umbrella Churches Together for a sizeable town (Appendix III(b)). The questions and the guidelines are offered to those seeking to set up a Churches Together grouping where there has been no formal structure as well as to those changing from Council of Churches mode.*

### 1. BASIS

Are we prepared to adopt the Churches Together in England Basis (see Basis)?

### 2. AIMS

Do all prospective members share the ecumenical vision spelt out in the Aims? Do we want to change the emphasis somewhat? Have we in spelling out the Aims in the "In particular ......" section managed to avoid undue overlap with the proper agenda of neighbourhood ecumenical groupings?

### 3. AREA

Have we got the **area** right? Does it follow civic boundaries? Does it split Catholic parishes? Should it include neighbouring villages?

### 4. RELATIONSHIPS

Have we liaised with our County Ecumenical Officer? Are we going to send agendas and minutes to the County Ecumenical Officer? Are we on the mailing list for ecumenical newsletter and CTE's *Pilgrim Post*?

### 5. MEMBERSHIP

Have we approached all the denominations in the locality? In category (a)? In category (b)? In category (c)? (see Appendix III(b) Membership). It is not a good witness if some denominations take a step to deeper commitment and others are marginalised. If some are hesitant, or dismissive, try to find out why. What is this telling us? Are they at least supportive of us in what we are doing? How can we develop relationships with them? Are we in touch with all the neighbourhood Churches Together groupings in our geographical area? Are there Christian organisations or projects in the locality which are not churches? As long as **most** of the members are churches, to include such groups will be an enrichment to the life of the Churches Together.

## 6. OFFICERS

These guidelines are self explanatory.

## 7. FORUM

What size of Forum are we looking for? Is there to be an Enabling Group/ Executive as well, in which case the Forum could be larger?

## 8. ENABLING GROUP/EXECUTIVE

Should the churches be asked to appoint one representative each or should the Forum elect out of the total representation? How big should it be? A tight group may make for efficiency, a large one be more representative.

## 9. FINANCE

What level of funding do we need? What expectations are there? Will churches be challenged to provide extra funding for specific events or projects? Should larger denominations be expected to pay more? Should subscriptions be based on total membership in the area covered, rather than on number of representatives appointed? Have we an auditor who is external to the local churches?

## 10. CONSTITUTION

Has the draft been approved by all the prospective Member Churches?

## 11. REVIEW

Have we lodged a copy of the adopted Constitution with the County Ecumenical Officer? Does each church have a copy of the Constitution in its own Records?

## III(b) DRAFT CONSTITUTIONAL GUIDELINES FOR AN UMBRELLA CHURCHES TOGETHER FOR A SIZEABLE TOWN WHICH HAS NEIGHBOURHOOD CHURCHES TOGETHER GROUPS WITHIN ITS AREA

*This document is to be regarded as advisory only and not definitive. Comments are welcomed. You are advised to consult your County Ecumenical Officer before adopting a Churches Together in .......... & District Constitution and to send him/her a copy of the final document. Please also send a copy of the document to the appropriate Field Officer of Churches Together in England.*

**BASIS**

CHURCHES TOGETHER IN .......... & District unites in pilgrimage those Churches in .......... & District which, acknowledging God's revelation in Christ, confess the Lord Jesus Christ as God and Saviour according to the Scriptures, and, in obedience to God's will and in the power of the Holy Spirit commit themselves

– to seek a deepening of their communion with Christ and with one another in the Church, which is His body; and

– to fulfil their mission to proclaim the Gospel by common witness and service in the world

to the glory of the one God, Father, Son and Holy Spirit.

**AIMS**

The aims of Churches Together in .......... & District shall be –

(a) to enable the churches, as pilgrims together, to explore the Christian faith together, to develop mutual relationships, to seek a common mind, and to make decisions together;

(b) to encourage churches to worship, pray and reflect together on the nature and purpose of the church in the light of its mission – each church sharing with others the treasures of its tradition;

(c) to enable the churches to live and share the Gospel, to evangelise together and to take further steps towards fuller unity;

(d) to enable the churches to respond to the needs of society and to witness to the Gospel together.

In particular Churches Together in .......... & District shall seek to –

i) serve as a means of communication between churches and neighbourhood Churches Together groups   within its area;

ii) provide induction courses as appropriate for ministers and clergy moving into the area;

iii) provide a focus for relating to the local authority and other statutory or voluntary bodies;

iv) co-ordinate church involvement in town twinning schemes;

v) co-ordinate mission and evangelism as appropriate across .......... & District

> (See Note 1)

## AREA

Churches Together in ......... & District aims to serve either the neighbourhood of .......... & District or an area coterminous with ........... local government area. (See attached map)

## RELATIONSHIPS

Churches Together in .......... & District is in association with ........ County Ecumenical Council/Sponsoring Body/Churches Together in ........ County. (See Note 2)

## MEMBERSHIP

Membership of Churches Together in .......... & District shall be open to –

(a) any church or association of local churches within one Christian tradition which is affiliated to a church or association of churches which is a full member of Churches Together in England (See Notes 3 & 5) **and**

(b) any church or association of local churches within one Christian tradition which affirms the Basis and commits itself to promote the aims of Churches Together in ........... & District and which has its own national or regional organisation and ecclesial identity (See Notes 4 & 5) **and**

(c) any church which on principle has no credal statements in its tradition and therefore cannot formally subscribe to the statement of faith in the Basis provided that it satisfies 75% in number of those full member churches which subscribe to the Basis that it manifests faith in Christ as witnessed to in the Scriptures and it is committed to the aims and purposes of Churches Together in ........... & District and that it will work in the spirit of the Basis (See Notes 5 & 6)

**and**

(d) any association, network, movement or ecumenical partnership which brings together Christians of different denominations in the area for purposes congruent with the basis and aims of Churches Together in .......... (See Notes 7, 8 & 9)

## OFFICERS

The officers of Churches Together in .......... & District shall be a Moderator and Deputy Moderator (one of whom shall normally be a minister and the other a lay person), an Honorary Treasurer and an Honorary Secretary (plus a Minute Secretary, if desired) to be elected at the Annual Meeting of the Forum. Officers shall serve for an initial period of (3) years and may be re-elected if willing to serve for one further period not exceeding (3) years.

## FORUM

(a) The Forum shall consist of –

either the clergy and ministers and up to... others from each participating church

or

....representatives of each member church under **MEMBERSHIP** (a), (b) and (c) and one representative of each member body under **MEMBERSHIP** (d) above. (See Notes 10 & 11)

(b) The Forum may co-opt others with particular expertise or understanding to bring. Co-options shall total not more than one quarter of the representatives elected to the Council and shall normally be for a maximum of two years. Those co-opted may not vote on amendments to the Constitution.

(c) The Forum shall meet not less than twice annually. The ...... (specify month or season) meeting shall be the Annual Meeting at which the audited accounts shall be presented, officers elected and annual reports submitted.

## ENABLING GROUP/EXECUTIVE

(a) The churches shall appoint an Enabling Group/Executive whose functions shall be to enable the member churches to make decisions in common and to serve as a reference point for the Forum.

(b) The Enabling Group/Executive shall comprise the officers of the Forum, up to four lay representatives, and up to four clergy or ministers appointed by the member churches with regard to an appropriate representation of the various Christian traditions and denominations in membership, and up to two representatives of category (d) MEMBERSHIP. (See Note 11)

(c)The Enabling Group/Executive may set up working groups to explore issues identified by the Forum or the Enabling Group/Executive. It may also commission a particular member church or body to work on behalf of all.

## FINANCE

Each member church and member body shall pay such annual sum to Churches Together in .......... & District as shall be agreed at the Annual Meeting of the Forum. The financial year shall be from .... (specify month) to ..... (specify month). Cheques shall require the signature of any of two of the four officers. An honorary auditor shall be appointed at the Annual Meeting.

## CONSTITUTION

The constitution and any subsequent amendment to it requires the approval of 75% of the member churches, acting through their normal decision-making bodies. (See Note 12).

## REVIEW

It is intended that Churches Together in .......... & District shall reflect the developing life of the Christian Churches as they continue their pilgrimage together. From time to time (every ... years) a Review Group shall be appointed by the member churches in consultation with the County Ecumenical Officer/County Sponsoring Body/Churches Together in ........ County to report on the progress of its pilgrimage and to make proposals for desirable changes.

## NOTES

1.This may involve such tasks as producing and updating a directory of churches and church-related organisations in the area, encouraging the development of inter-faith dialogue; finding appropriate church representation from committees or working parties involving statutory, private and voluntary sectors, e.g. in relation to Single Regeneration Budget bids and projects.

2.Check with the CTE Field Officer whether there is an ecumenical body covering your County or City region. If not, the following may be substituted as Article 5 in the Constitution:–

"Churches Together in ..... and District is in association with Churches Together in England".

3. A list of the member churches of Churches Together in England is given in Appendix II(b)

4. Churches Together in England is open to receive applications for membership from other churches. Some local churches, which will on principle be unwilling to become a member of a national body because of their understanding of the church as local, may be willing to become members of local Churches Together groups. In each case a judgement will have to be made as to whether membership of an umbrella Churches Together is appropriate.

5. This form of words is appropriate for a body where the emphasis will be on denominational representation rather than representation from each local church.

6. Upon its inauguration Churches Together in England welcomed the Religious Society of Friends under clause 6 above.

7. This may include neighbourhood Churches Together groups, local or wider ecumenical partnerships, and agencies such as Christian Aid and CAFOD.

8. As at January 1998 the member bodies in association with Churches Together in England were –

Afro-West Indian United Council of Churches

Association of Interchurch Families

Bible Society

Christians Aware

The College of Preachers

The Fellowship of Prayer for Unity

Iona Community

National Association of Christian Communities and Networks (NACCAN)

National Retreat Association

Student Christian Movement

The Focolare Movement

Young Men's Christian Association

Young Women's Christian Association

9. In the case of a town or city-wide grouping of Churches Together, attention is drawn to *Free Church Councils in the 90s*, a discussion document available from Free Churches' Council, 27 Tavistock Square, London WC1 9HH. This suggests constitutional guidelines by which the Free Church members of a local council of churches (and, by extension, a Churches Together in ..........) may constitute the Free Church Council in ..........

If there is already a distinct Free Church Council in existence in .........., negotiation should take place to discover whether the pattern which integrates the life of the Free Church Council within an ecumenical grouping with a wider membership is acceptable.

10. It may be desirable to relate the number of representatives on the Forum to the denominational membership or number of congregations in the area served. It may also be desirable to specify church 'leaders' who should by virtue of their office have a right to a seat on the Forum and/or the Enabling Group/Executive (e.g. Provost, (Rural) Dean, Circuit Superintendent).

11.It will usually be desirable to accord direct membership under category (d) to each neighbourhood Churches Together group. The balance between denominational representation and neighbourhood Churches Together group representation on the Forum and on the Enabling Group/Executive will need to be carefully thought through.

12. It cannot be over-emphasised that a major principle of the new ecumenical process is that it is the churches' own decision-making bodies, rather than simply a representative council acting on behalf of the churches, which need to make major ecumenical decisions about policy and priorities.

*TAILPIECE* .....

## TEN COMMANDMENTS FOR THE NEXT PHASE OF ECUMENISM

❶ Worship is central, therefore always ask what is the adequacy of our offering to God.

❷ Keep asking the biggest, hardest questions, and don't be put off by trivialities.

❸ Never impute worse motives to other churches than to your own.

❹ Keep in the heart of ecumenism the needs of the world and the suffering of so many.

❺ Remember that ecumenism is a movement, not a competing institution.

❻ Hold unity and diversity together in your planning and your prayers.

❼ Our future is more important than our past; that is the meaning of forgiveness

❽ Don't allow the financial and legal experts to determine the policy, but to serve it.

❾ Listen to the young, the outsiders, the non-experts as well as the professionals.

❿ Never give up!

*Bernard Thorogood, former General Secretary of the United Reformed Church.*

# INDEX OF PLACE NAMES IN ENGLAND

# INFORMATION AND ADDRESSES

## CHURCHES TOGETHER IN ENGLAND

Member Churches are listed on page 92.

Member Bodies in Association are listed on page 99.

Agencies of Churches Together in England:

CAFOD, 2 Romero Close, Stockwell Road, London SW9 9TY.

Christian Aid, PO Box 100 London SE1 7RL.

Christian Enquiry Agency, Inter-Church House, 35-41 Lower Marsh, London SE1 7RL.

Churches Advisory Council for Local Broadcasting, PO Box 124, Westcliff on Sea, Essex SS0 0QU.

Opportunities for Volunteering, Inter-Church House, 35-41 Lower Marsh, London SE1 7RL.

## OTHER USEFUL ADDRESSES

CCBI, Inter-Church House, 35-41 Lower Marsh, London SE1 7RL.

Christian Ecology Link, 20 Carlton Road, Harrogate HG2 8DD.

Christians for Social Justice, 31 Prince of Wales Lane, Yardley Road, Birmingham B14 4LB.

Church Action on Disability, Charisma Cottage, Drewsteignton, Exeter, EX6 6QR.

Churches & Blindness, Mrs. R. Curtis, Dippers, Water Lane, Charlton Horethorne, Sherborne, DT9 4NX.

Churches Commission for Racial Justice, Inter-Church House, 35-41 Lower Marsh, London SE1 7RL.

Fellowship of Reconciliation, 40-46 Harleyford Road, Vauxhall, London SE11 5AY.

One World Week, PO Box 2555, Reading, Berks., RG1 4XW.

Quaker Peace and Service, Friends House, Euston Road, London NW1 2BJ.

Roman Catholic Justice & Peace Commission, 39 Eccleston Square, London SW1V 1PD.

Tear Fund (The Evangelical Alliance Relief Fund), 100 Church Road, Teddington, TW11 8QE.

The Lifestyle Movement, 21 Fleetwood Court, West Byfleet, Surrey KT14 6BE.

Women's Environmental Network, 287 City Road, London EC1V 1LA.

World Development Movement, 25 Beehive Place, London SW9 7QR.